Penguin Books

Believe and Achieve!

Paul Hanna is one of Australia's leading motivational speakers, with a client list that is a who's who of Australian business – Toyota, Optus, Westpac, Qantas, Aussie Home Loans, BMW and Colonial are a few of the leading corporations who have used the services of this dynamic young speaker. McDonald's Australia, regarded by many as the leader in 'people development', have had more than 5000 staff attend Paul's full-day seminar.

Paul's presentations focus on the individual achieving more of his or her potential, with his audiences loving his low-key, no-hype approach. He has been speaking professionally for more than a decade, and is the bestselling author of *You Can Do It!*, *The Mini Motivator* and *The Money Motivator*.

Paul lives in Sydney.

What readers have said about Paul Hanna

I am a 24-year-old office manager/secretary to the director of a small but very successful mortgage lending company ... After reading your book, I am now very focused and believe I will have a lot of happiness and success in my life in the years to come. Thank you for making me so happy that I feel I could burst.

Renee, Bentleigh, Victoria

Among the many motivation-type books published to date, only a few provide practical advice, since the majority of them are just filled with abstract concepts. You Can Do It! is one of the few truly authentic books and the messages penetrate right into the heart of readers. Unlike the messages that are deduced from the so-called grand theories up in the air in most of the books, your advice is not mere speculation. It has already been tested either by you or by your clients.

Noriaki, Yamanashi-ken, Japan

I have just finished reading your extraordinary book *You Can Do It!* for the second time. Your book has given me some inspiration to kickstart my path into rebuilding my life again after a traumatic 14 years. I am 31 years old and the past few months have seen me at the end of my rope, ready to give up on life because I did not have the courage or strength to deal with any more hardships ... I only wish I had stumbled across your book earlier. I congratulate you on your capacity to help other people in their endeavour to pick themselves up out of damaging thought patterns they create for themselves and lead them into a path of self-love and determination to change their lives for the better.

Sally, Hinchinbrook, New South Wales

I'm a 22-year-old university student and am writing to tell you how much I enjoyed and have learnt from your book You Can Do It! *I am currently reading it for the second time and am finding it to be as inspirational as the first time I read it. I believe I have become a stronger person from reading this book, as I have now learnt to take control of the things that happen in my life, rather than leaving it up to other people to decide what will happen ... I have never written a letter like this before, but then again, never have I been so moved or inspired by a book before! Thank you Paul, you have made a huge impact on my life.*

Georgette, Bateau Bay, New South Wales

You have inspired and helped me tremendously. My life was falling apart but with determination and your book *You Can Do It!* I have changed and my self-esteem is growing.

Rod, The Rock, New South Wales

I found reading your book motivated me, but being really hyped up and motivated at 11.30 p.m. doesn't achieve much when you need to sleep. Instead I started to read you on the bus to work. This way I felt totally hyped on arrival at work and throughout the day. I even carry The Mini Motivator *with me. You never know when you'll need a hit of Paul Hanna to tide you over!*

Gail, Dee Why, New South Wales

Since your book *You Can Do It!* was given to me a week ago I haven't been able to put it down. I would just like to say how inspirational your book has been (no other book I have read has affected me so) and how it has made me look at my life in a more positive way and made me understand and believe that I can do it . . . Having lost my mother a couple of months ago after a year-long battle with cancer, my personal life and work had taken quite a hammering. A very astute friend gave me your book to read, and here I am! **Thank you** for an unexpected Christmas gift.

Caterina, Hallett Cove, South Australia

I was speechless after reading your book You Can Do It! *You are an inspiration. What an unbelievable world it would be if everybody read your book. I recently bought another copy to give to a close friend and will continue to buy it as a present as I believe it is the best gift you could give anyone.*

Kit, Richmond, Victoria

Thank you! I recently cruised into a book shop and asked for guidance from the universe to choose a book I need at the moment. Well, haven't you put a lot of questions I have been asking myself into perspective! I'm loaded with enthusiasm, potential and questions, Paul. I think you're pretty cool. Thank you for your dynamic reinforcement, your time to produce a book we need and for your encouragement.

Emma-Jane, South Yarra, Victoria

I read your book You Can Do It! *yesterday and it literally blew me away. I've read a number of self-development books over the years, but yours has had a profound impact on me and made me realise a lot of things about myself . . . I'm sure you've helped a great number of people re-evaluate their lives. This is your gift to society.*

Ellie, Leura, New South Wales

What business has said about Paul Hanna

With more than 3000 of our management, employees and dealer staff having attended Paul's seminars, it's no wonder his name keeps coming up every time 'attitude and high performance' are discussed. With the success of *You Can Do It!* and *The Mini Motivator*, Paul has not only endeared himself to Toyota, but also to the many thousands of readers who, like us, enjoy his down-to-earth communication style. More than anything else, what leaves a lasting impression is Paul's ability to challenge you to believe that you can achieve more of your potential.

Tom Phillips
Director, Sales and Marketing, Toyota Motor Corporation Australia

I'm delighted to pen a few words in support of Paul Hanna's latest book. Paul has motivated over 5000 members of our restaurant management team through very simple yet effective messages and stories. He causes all of us to challenge ourselves, to do better, to try harder and to enjoy what we do. This latest work you could say is more of the same, only better – which also reflects each encounter I have with Paul.

Charlie Bell
Managing Director/CEO, McDonald's Australia

At Aussie, we have had more than 3000 of our employees and clients attend Paul Hanna's seminar. Paul is a gifted and articulate speaker, and his latest book is essential reading. You will enjoy his straightforward and down-to-earth approach.

John Symond
Managing Director, Aussie Home Loans

Paul Hanna is a breath of fresh air. He brings simplicity to bear on complex issues with surprising results.

John D. Malouf
Chief Operating Officer, AGC Limited

If you're serious about getting the results you want in your life, get this book. Paul Hanna is a master at what really counts – getting results. He has a rare ability to eliminate distractions and get you working on the things that matter. And most importantly, he shows you how much fun the journey can be. *Believe and Achieve!* is a 'must read'.

John McGrath
Managing Director, McGrath Partners Estate Agents

Paul Hanna showed us the way with his bestseller You Can Do It! – *what a great follow-up* Believe and Achieve! *is. And there is no better example than Paul Hanna himself. Congratulations, Paul – success follows success.*

Wayne Handley
Managing Director, Lend Lease Financial Planning

Whenever we conduct training sessions on ways to improve our overall performance, Paul Hanna's name is mentioned. Paul has had an enormous impact on our staff. His technique in convincing people to set their goals and ensure they follow through is remarkable. Our staff constantly refer to Paul's first book, *You Can Do It!*, whenever they need a reminder that they can achieve more.

Peter Capp
Head of Financial Planning and Investment Sales, Colonial

Paul has played a major role in building the self-esteem of our sales force – the most critical component for success in any endeavour. Paul's catch-cry, 'Your attitude determines your altitude', is well known throughout our company. And a glance at that '747' has jolted many of our people to refocus skywards, lifting their expectations and moving towards their original goals and dreams.

Ken Wright
General Manager, Investments and Insurance, Westpac

Paul has already reset many 'cruising altitudes' through his seminars and books, with resultant personal and corporate growth. Now *Believe and Achieve!* will ensure that we focus and take control of the right flight path for a successful entry into the new millennium.

Howard Davy
National Manager, National Mutual Financial Services

Paul Hanna is Australia's leading 'Getting your act into gear' consultant. He doesn't just talk about being a positive thinker – he shows you how you can turn your life around at home and at work. He will show you the easy steps to believing, so you can unlock the door to achieving!

Robin Honeychurch
Zone Manager, SA & NT, AMP Financial Services

Also by Paul Hanna

You Can Do It!
The Mini Motivator
The Money Motivator

Believe and Achieve!

Paul Hanna

PENGUIN BOOKS

Penguin Books Australia Ltd
487 Maroondah Highway, PO Box 257
Ringwood, Victoria 3134, Australia
Penguin Books Ltd
Harmondsworth, Middlesex, England
Penguin Putnam Inc.
375 Hudson Street, New York, New York 10014, USA
Penguin Books Canada Limited
10 Alcorn Avenue, Toronto, Ontario, Canada M4V 3B2
Penguin Books (NZ) Ltd
Cnr Rosedale and Airborne Roads, Albany, Auckland, New Zealand
Penguin Books (South Africa) (Pty) Ltd
5 Watkins Street, Denver Ext 4, 2094, South Africa
Penguin Books India (P) Ltd
11, Community Centre, Panchsheel Park, New Delhi 110 017, India

First published by Penguin Books Australia Ltd 1998

10 9 8 7 6 5

Cover design by Guy Mirabella
Typeset in Times and Frutiger by Midland Typesetters, Maryborough, Victoria
Printed in Australia by Australian Print Group, Maryborough, Victoria

National Library of Australia
Cataloguing-in-Publication data:

Hanna, Paul, 1960– .
  Believe and achieve!

  ISBN 0 14 027244 5.

  1. Success. 2. Motivation (Psychology). I. Title.

158.1

www.penguin.com.au

JOHN DENVER

1943–97

*This book is dedicated to John Denver.
His songs inspired me in the early days of my business,
when I didn't believe I would achieve my dreams.
He proved by his legacy that we can all make a difference.*

Contents

Preface

You Have to First Believe, Before You Can Achieve

Believe and Achieve! is about first knowing that you deserve to be successful, and then learning the tools and techniques to attract success to yourself, easily and effortlessly.

While I was writing *Believe and Achieve!*, I received what I call a 'wake-up call'. A normal wake-up call is when you are woken up from sleep at a time of your choosing, but the wake-up call I am talking about was a metaphorical one – the kind you don't specifically ask for, but which turns out to be your greatest 'teacher'.

My 'wake-up call' came just before Christmas last year, when my mum was critically injured in a head-on collision with a drunk driver. I learnt first-hand and in a very painful way that it's easy to say 'believe and achieve', but it's another thing to put it into action. When my family were all gathered around Mum's hospital bed and it looked like death was near, I realised this was the time to dig as deep as I could to find the courage to believe she was going to pull through. I also saw that my belief in myself determined whether I really believed she would live.

So How is *Believe and Achieve!* Different to *You Can Do It!*?

While *You Can Do It!* provided the foundation for your goals, *Believe and Achieve!* builds on that foundation, providing you with more powerful case studies and tools to help take you to the next 'altitude'. While writing *You Can Do It!* I was mindful of the need to produce a book that was not only easy to read, but also easy to finish. This meant that a lot of the material I wanted to share in *You Can Do It!* had to be held over to *Believe and Achieve!* This has worked out really well, because many of the people who read my first book have asked to be taken higher and further in the next one.

'Non-attachment' is one area that will take you to new heights in your search for a calmer, more relaxed lifestyle. 'The gift of setbacks' is another chapter every reader will relate to. It's about how your attitude to these setbacks will ultimately determine whether you grow and learn from them or become a victim of them.

I want *Believe and Achieve!* to challenge you to new 'altitudes'. I want to ignite those dreams which, for whatever reason, have been smothered by negativity, loneliness or by you simply losing focus because you are trying to cope with today's hectic lifestyle.

As a famous tennis star once said, 'You don't win Wimbledon, then believe you're an awesome tennis star.' You first have to believe, and then you will achieve.

With kind regards,
Paul Hanna
Sydney, Australia

Introduction

Everyone wants to make a difference in this world; to put their very own stamp on this wonderful planet and make a contribution.

When you are growing up, you dream of going to the places you learn about in school. You see a bright red sports car and whisper to yourself that one day you'll get one just like it. Or after seeing a romantic film, you walk out of the cinema declaring that you will find your perfect partner, just like in the movie.

What happens along the way? Somehow you lose your capacity to believe you can achieve your dreams. You start to believe that the future is not as wonderful as when you were a kid. You get conditioned to accept second-best. The people around you say things like, 'Be happy with what you've got; there are people far worse off than you.' The people who make such comments mean well, but they actually have no idea how life works.

I consult with some of the leading businesspeople in Australia, and all of them are generous to charities. There's no way they could donate hundreds of thousands of dollars to charity if they were not successful and focused. Nor could they be in a position to employ thousands of Australians. Instead of being content to cruise along in life and not challenge themselves, they have forged ahead on their own and made a contribution to Australian life. Every successful person I know has used the tried and proven techniques outlined in *Believe and Achieve!* Some of the techniques are new and others are more than 2000 years old. If you want to improve a particular area of your life, keep reading, because I know you will find at least one tool or technique which could transform you. And that's all you need! If you get just one tip from this book to help you along your path to success, then it was worth the investment.

Since the launch in 1997 of *You Can Do It!*, I have been overwhelmed by thousands of messages of gratitude from readers in every corner of Australia. Some letters brought me to tears because of the sheer struggle the reader had endured up to that point in their life. Others made me laugh with joy because after reading my book, the person had found 'the missing link' which has since propelled them to meteoric success in their home and work life.

I have particularly enjoyed writing *Believe and Achieve!* because my readers have assisted me in topic choice and style. It is they who made *You Can Do It!* a national number-one bestseller and for that I am eternally grateful. *The Mini Motivator*, a pocket motivational book launched six months after *You Can Do It!*, also became a bestseller, which truly humbled me. The success of the books, and the fact that my seminars in corporate Australia were fully booked months ahead, led me to think, 'Hey, I'm doing all right!' But at the same time I let my health slip to the point where I was visiting a chiropractor at least once a week. I suddenly saw how I was caught at my own 'cruising altitude'; how I had got used to the level I was flying at.

Since then, I haven't been to the chiropractor nearly as much; in fact, I've only been half a dozen times in the last 12 months! In *Believe and Achieve!* I want to share with you how I lost 18 kilos and returned to the energy levels I had five years ago, all without spending one cent. I want to share how my seminars have gone through the roof with my new-found energy and lighter body shape.

Believe and Achieve! is all about getting back to basics and becoming more focused about what you want to achieve in life. It's about not accepting other people's conditioning of you and believing in your goals. More than anything else, *Believe and Achieve!* is about assisting you to get that spark back into your life and achieve your dreams.

Believe in you

Whatever the mind can conceive and believe,
it can achieve.

NAPOLEON HILL

In this chapter:

- ◆ Your beliefs about you determine your success in life

  Field of Dreams – if you believe, it will happen

  How I overcame setbacks in my business

  The world is reflecting how you feel about yourself

  The Man in the Mirror – you will never forget it

- ◆ How your self-image can be your friend or your foe

  How your attitude determines your altitude

  Letting go of put-downs

- ◆ Why stirrers are people with low self-esteem

- ◆ Being an optimist is hard work

  The technique sportspeople use to stay on top

  The Optimists' Creed

I f you truly want to achieve more than you are currently achieving, then before you do anything else you need to lift your belief in yourself.

I think we all believe in ourselves to some degree or another – but it's *to what degree* that this book is all about. It's your opinion of yourself that got you here in the first place. This might sound quite strange at first, but hang in with me and I will show you what I mean.

Everything you have accomplished up to this point has been evaluated and processed by your self-image, or opinion of yourself. Likewise, every opportunity you have missed out on has been processed by your self-image and rejected as too good for you!

As crazy as this might sound, it's true. Your self-image has been programmed by you to look for achievement and success at a certain level. It rejects anything it sees as 'not good enough' for you, which is fine – but it also rejects incidents and people that could take your life up to a completely new level in every area: financial, emotional, physical and spiritual.

Belief in Yourself Doesn't Happen Overnight

It would be great if there was an instant, magic 'Hey presto!' way of increasing your belief in yourself – but the fact is, it has to be built upon bit by bit, one step at a time.

When I started speaking professionally ten years ago, I learnt very painfully how much other people did or did not believe in me. I also realised how much I did not really believe in my own capabilities. I was in a fantastic job, travelling around the world designing holidays which Australians would eventually book 12 months later. It was a job that made me see myself as a 'world member'. I always used to get 'butterflies' before I boarded a 747 to somewhere – because of excitement, not nerves! But ten years ago I had just turned 27, and I knew there was more for me to achieve out there.

So the leap to start my own business was a crucial one. I'm so glad I started it when I did, because I really had no idea how hard it was going to be. I was young and naive and bursting at the seams with enthusiasm – but if I had known what was coming, I would have stayed in my old job.

Field of Dreams – Believe and It Will Come

After more than two years of struggle to get my business off the ground, and a growing debt to pay, my confidence was slowly being eaten away. I was being hassled by everyone – the bank because of the debt, my family because they thought I was throwing good money away, and my friends because they thought I had tossed in a great job for nothing. The bank manager didn't give a damn; he just wanted his money back. Every time I said, 'It's just about to take off,' he would reply, 'Paul, you've been saying that for two years now.'

I was learning very quickly that life in your own business is not all peaches and cream. It's bloody tough, and no one really understands how you are feeling. Things were pretty bad when I received a call from the bank manager to say that I had two weeks to reduce my debt by $10 000 or the bank would 'take action'. I knew this was crunch time. The bank wasn't going to take any more 'It's coming' stories. They wanted proof that my business was developing, and in the words of Cuba Gooding Jnr in the film *Jerry McGuire*, they wanted me to 'show them the money!'

One evening, I decided to take in a movie. I was feeling cornered in every direction and couldn't see my way out of the mess I had put myself in, and thought that going to a movie might cheer me up and get me motivated. As it happened, the local cinema was showing Kevin Costner's *Field of Dreams*, which is about believing in yourself when everyone around you is doubting you. Could I relate with this, or what?!

In the movie, Kevin Costner has the bank, his brother-in-law and nearly everyone else against him. He wants to build a baseball stadium on his cornfield in memory of his father, but to achieve this dream he risks losing everything, including the family farm. He keeps waking up during the night to hear a voice saying, 'If you build it, they will come.'

I came out of the movie crying – not because of sadness, but because I had realised that **'If I built it, they would come'** in my business too. *Field of Dreams* changed the way I thought about myself and my business forever. Like the main character, I had the bank and family and friends starting to doubt me. What I realised after seeing the movie was that the people around me couldn't possibly believe in my dreams as much as I did, because they couldn't see what I was seeing.

I walked home that night feeling on top of the world. The corner I thought I had backed myself into was really the start of the success of my business. The bad situation I was in had nothing to do with the bank or my family and friends. It was about belief in my dreams and goals. It was about believing in me.

The Deal Comes Through

You will recall that the bank had given me an ultimatum. Around that time I had a prospective client in Canberra, Bob, who was giving me every excuse why he could not do business with me. And I was taking it. What he was really asking was why he *should* do business with me – and I couldn't give him a decent response. He wanted me to convince him, with passion, why he should spend $15 000 to train his employees.

After watching *Field of Dreams*, I rang Bob and said I had to see him urgently. I flew to Canberra and told him about the movie. Bob was impressed. He said it sounded like just what he needed at the moment, and that he would go and see *Field of Dreams* that Saturday evening. Before I left his office, I said, 'If I can do you a great deal, can we do business?'

I told him that if he wrote me a cheque right there and then, I would give him an excellent deal. After haggling for a while, we agreed on $10 000. I returned to Sydney that night and deposited the cheque the next morning, much to my bank manager's surprise.

Can you believe that? After months of mucking around and delays, I had finally started to believe in myself. And straight away, my business was off the ground. This was not only a turning point for me; my bank manager started to see that I wasn't all hot air and talk after all. There *were* clients and there *was* business.

The World is Reflecting You

Bob rang me the next Sunday morning to say how much he had enjoyed the movie and that he was really looking forward to the seminars I would be doing for his organisation. As you can imagine, seeing *Field of Dreams* and then landing the deal with Bob had been a belief-changing experience for me. After his phone call,

I reflected how easy life could be if **I changed the way I saw the world, and did not wait for the world to change**.

In *You Can Do It!* I featured the following poem, which was given to me by a seminar attendee many years ago. I have had so much feedback from readers that I feel I must share it with you again. The story behind it is about two men on death row in California, just about to be executed. After the executions, the prison guards were cleaning the cell that both prisoners had shared the night before – their last night on earth. To the guards' amazement, they found this poem inscribed on the cell wall.

The Man in the Mirror

When you get what you want in your struggle for self
And the world makes you King for a day
Then go to the mirror and look at yourself
And see what the Man has to say

For it isn't a man's father, mother or wife
Whose judgement upon him must pass
The fellow whose verdict counts most in his life
Is the Man staring back from the glass

He's the fellow to please, never mind all the rest
For he's with you clear up to the end
And you've passed your most dangerous, difficult test
If the Man in the glass is your friend

You can fool the whole world down the pathway of years
And get pats on the back as you pass
But your final reward will be heartache and tears
If you've cheated the Man in the glass

Your Self-image – Friend or Foe?

Maxwell Maltz, in his amazing book *Psycho Cybernetics*, proved that your self-image is the maker or breaker of your life. How you see yourself determines more than anything else how you treat the world, and this then determines what you attract in your world.

When he wrote the book, Maltz was a leading American plastic surgeon. What led him to research the topic of self-image was the feedback he received from patients after he had operated on them. On many occasions, when their bandages were removed, they would be very upset because they said they couldn't see any difference in their appearance.

Maltz was flabbergasted. He could easily see the changes that had occurred, and knew exactly what cosmetic work – which in many cases was quite substantial – had been done. Even when they had seen the 'before/after' photos, many patients felt they were walking out of his surgery 'unchanged'. Maltz realised that while he had altered the patients' physical features, the unhappy ones had not 'operated within' to change how they saw themselves – their own self-image.

Your self-image can be your friend, propelling you to unbelievable success – or it can keep you in the depths of despair. It all comes back to how you see yourself.

What Opinions are You Reinforcing of Yourself?

In *You Can Do It!*, I compared self-image to the autopilot of a 747 jumbo jet. The autopilot has been given instructions to fly at a cruising altitude of, say, 35 000 feet. When the pilots are in the air, they activate the autopilot and the 747 obeys the instructions by flying at the programmed height. If the radar detects rough weather ahead, the pilots have two choices. They can override the autopilot and fly above the rough weather, or they can put completely new information into the autopilot – say 50 000 feet – and fly at a higher altitude permanently.

You face this dilemma every day, where the autopilot is your self-image and the 'rough weather' is something in your life upsetting you. If you are flying at a higher altitude, it makes sense that you won't run into as much rough weather as when you are flying at a lower altitude. When you are under stress, you can 'grab the controls' and try to fly higher for a while, or you can reprogram your autopilot – your self-image – with new information to keep you up at the higher altitude full-time.

There is an old saying that goes: '**If you keep on doing today what you have always done, you will only get tomorrow what you have always got.**' In other words, if you are not completely thrilled with how things are going, and want something better in a particular area of your life, it stands to reason that you will have to change your thinking in that area to effect any form of change. If you keep on speaking to yourself the way you are, it's logical to accept that you will stay at the same cruising altitude you are at now.

No More Put-downs from Now On

At a seminar in Brisbane, I met Rick. He was flabbergasted at how one single point could have such a major impact on his life. He told me he had nearly fallen off his chair when I said: '**Stirrers are people with low self-esteem**.'

Rick said that up till then he had thought he was a positive type of person, the kind who is always 'having a go' at people at work and at home, getting a few laughs here and there. What he didn't realise was that the laughs he got were coming at the expense of the people around him – his colleagues, his wife and his kids. Rick said that he now understood why his kids were not doing very well in school. It was because he was always 'cutting them down to size', or in other words creating an atmosphere where his kids felt hopeless and therefore ended up with poor self-esteem.

Missed Promotions Now Explained

Rick had not only discovered how his stirring was causing problems at home; he realised that his own low self-esteem was holding him back at work. Over the last two years, he had noticed that he always made the 'short list' for a promotion, but when it came down to the wire someone else always got the job. Every time, he was told that he was 'just unlucky' to have missed out.

Rick knew he was good at his job, and these missed promotions were really starting to get him down. He said, 'Now at last I know why. If I take total accountability for my life, both at home and at work, I can start concentrating on my performance instead of cutting other people down.'

The Wedding Anniversary that Had Bells Ringing

Rick's learning curve did not end at the seminar. The following weekend he was invited to his parents' home to a party to celebrate their thirtieth wedding anniversary. Rick noticed that for the whole evening, his father was cutting people down. He couldn't believe it. He had grown up in this environment and never noticed this trait in his father. And worse still, he now saw himself behaving in a very similar way.

After the party Rick was angry with his dad. He went into 'blame mode', blaming his father for how things had turned out. The anger only lasted 24 hours – and then he woke up to himself. He realised that his dad had most probably inherited the behaviour, in turn, from his own father, whom Rick could remember as a bit of a negative person. After this realisation, Rick became much more aware of how he himself had been cutting people down in the guise of joking or stirring.

But the best was yet to come. Rick wanted desperately to share this knowledge with his father, but he wanted to do it without hurting his dad's feelings. Rick had purchased my audio program of *You Can Do It!* and decided that the best way to open his father's mind to the new piece of information was to play the program to him. He came up with a plan. First, he invited his dad to join him and a mate, Jack, the next Sunday for a few rounds of golf near Jack's place on the Gold Coast. He knew his dad, who loves golf, would jump at the chance and he was right. Rick planned to play the program to his dad in the car on the way to the golf course. He didn't want to make his strategy too obvious, so he set the program to start at a point just before I talk about 'stirrers'.

When Sunday arrived, Rick picked his dad up and after a few kilometres, started playing the program. To his amazement, his dad remained silent for the next 20 minutes. The penny had dropped and his dad listened very intently to every word. Afterwards he told Rick that he was surprised to hear about himself, and shocked to think that people might not be as thrilled about the 'stirring' as he had thought – in fact, they might even be hurt by it. Rick said that his dad was now reading *You Can Do It!* and that he had never seen him so vibrant and positive.

Everyone Wants to Change

Rick's story is powerful because he not only took accountability to change his own performance, but also didn't make the easy mistake of blaming his dad for where he is today. Rick decided that when his dad was growing up he had not had the opportunity to hear this sort of information, and so did not really understand the damage he was doing. His father is now embracing the information with gusto.

How Many 'Stirrers' Do You Know?

Who do you know who could do with learning about this area? Which of your family members or friends is always cutting people down by stirring them?

Without doubt, every person I know who does this has a low opinion of themselves. They carry on with all the bravado in the world, and look as though they're having a great time, but underneath that 'fun' exterior, more often than not, is a person who is 'crying' inside. If their self-esteem improves, you'll see their 'stirring' habit subside.

If you know someone right now who fits this description, start working on their self-esteem by commenting on positive aspects of their performance. The rewards are well worth it, let me tell you!

Is Your Glass Half-full or Half-empty?

Are you an optimist or a pessimist? Some people say that optimists live in a fools' paradise, that they think everything is rosy and life is like Disneyland. These pessimists have made a commitment to themselves to walk around whingeing about where they are at in life. But this attitude achieves only one thing – it drags other people down.

Being an optimist is hard work. You need to have great self-discipline to call on when the going gets tough. And what do you need for great self-discipline? High self-esteem or self-worth. Being a pessimist is much easier, and that's why people with low self-esteem take the easy road. They know they won't be called on to use any self-discipline when something arrives in their life to challenge them.

Whatever You Can Believe, You Can Achieve

This is an old cliché, but it's so true. Optimists know that the key to staying on top of things is to make sure their self-image is constantly fed positive information. They know that just as they can become positive in an instant, their world can also be turned upside down if they let negative information infiltrate their self-talk.

Look at the many sportspeople who achieve success in one tournament and then, after a small loss or hiccup the following week, let their self-talk turn negative. And then? Nothing. They flounder at the bottom of the table of the sport where they were once a champion. I wonder why?

I know why. As much as they might be a champion golfer or tennis star, they are still *human beings* and as such still operate the way you and I do. In fact, in some ways it's harder for a top sports star to pick themselves up, because not only do they have their own self-talk criticising them, but they have the world's media bagging them as well. Making a mistake at work is tough enough, but can you imagine waking up the next morning to see it as the lead story in the morning newspaper? That's why I have so much praise and respect for sportspeople – like us, they have setbacks, but despite the constant negative messages bombarding them via the media, they manage to come back and perform.

If you think about it, you'll be amazed at how negative words have crept into your vocabulary over the years without you being consciously aware of them. For example, when you look at a glass of water, do you see it as half-full or half-empty? It's just a little thing, but it really gives you an idea of how you might be viewing.

Rainy Days Don't Have to Get You Down

Ted, a very successful businessman, had all his staff attend my half-day seminar. Ted said that one of the major influences in his life was his grandmother on his father's side: 'While she may have died when I was only ten, I can still remember her constant reassurances that things would always work out.'

One thing Ted still remembers vividly occurred on a rainy day during the school holidays. While everyone else, including the weather presenter on TV, was complaining about the wet, Ted's grandmother took him into town and walked him through the botanical gardens, explaining how important water was and its place in nature. Ted said, 'This was such a powerful lesson, at such an early age, that I am always reminded of it whenever there are challenges in my life – or whenever it rains!'

The Optimist's Creed

I have received a dazzling number of letters, faxes and phone calls since *You Can Do It!* was released. One reader sent me the following piece about optimists. Can you relate to it?

I promise:
- To be strong so that nothing can disturb my peace of mind
- To talk health, happiness and prosperity to every person I meet
- To make all my friends feel that there is something in them
- To look at the sunny side of everything and make my optimism come true
- To think only the best, work only for the best, and expect only the best
- To be just as enthusiastic about the success of others as I am about my own
- To forget the mistakes of the past and press on to greater achievements in the future
- To wear a cheerful countenance at all times and give every living creature I meet a smile
- To give so much time to the improvement of myself that I have no time to criticise others
- To be too large for worry, too noble for anger, too strong for fear and too happy to permit the presence of trouble

Want to know more about...?

2

Expect the best

Once you say you're going to settle for second-best,
that's what happens to you in life, I find.

JOHN F. KENNEDY

In this chapter:

- Why expecting the best usually attracts the best
- Letting go of the blame and hurt of the past
- No such thing as a born achiever
- The Self-esteem Bank Account
- Focusing on what you want, not on what you don't want
- Rear-vision thinking and hands-on-the-steering-wheel thinking
- Your subconscious can't tell what's real and what's pretend
- How you determine your crossbar of achievement

As I travel around Australia conducting my seminars, the following question is always asked, in one way or another: 'Paul, is there any one trait you notice in people who are achieving in their life?'

My answer is simple. Any person who is achieving success always expects the best to happen to them. They have harnessed a real, deep-seated belief in themselves so that whatever happens, they know they are going to win. They are so focused on the positive outcome that petty troubles don't seem to distract and upset them as much as they do other people. Successful people never lose sight of their dreams and goals and are always expecting the best.

It's Up to You

One of the first steps on the road to **believing you can achieve your dreams and goals** is to realise that no one can do it for you. You, and you alone, are in the pilot's seat of your life and only you can make the changes needed for your future happiness and success. There are literally thousands of books, tapes and seminars available to assist you in your journey, but nothing will change unless you start to expect the best in your life. And I don't mean just in your personal relationships or your work environment. I mean the total picture. Everything. When you expect only positive outcomes in your world, you create events around you to bring these positive events to pass. Likewise, if you expect less than the best in your life, you create a 'second-best' scenario and put yourself in places which cause you to achieve only mediocrity.

Now if you're thinking, 'We can't *all* win in life – *someone* has to lose', my question is, 'Why should it be you?'

I'm not saying, 'Stuff everyone else.' What I'm saying is, 'Why should you have to accept anything but the best in your life?' If there are people who want to accept second-best, let them have it, but you didn't invest in this book because you're satisfied with where you are at in life. You know you deserve more – and there's nothing wrong with that. And if, somewhere in your past, someone has told you there is something wrong with wanting more – toss that belief out now!

Remember, you can't give away something you don't already have. So if you lift your expectations and achieve more, you can give away heaps more love, friendship and material things to your family and friends.

You want to achieve more, and I congratulate you for that. Now it's time to focus on some very powerful tools and techniques that will change your world forever.

You Have Created Your World

The first and most important step in changing your future is to accept responsibility for where you are currently at. This is really important, because if you think that someone else is to blame for what is currently happening in your world, it will be very hard to move forward.

By your very own expectations in life, you have attracted the people and events in your life. You need to accept this major point before we can move on. Where are you blaming someone or something for the way you currently feel? Maybe it's a former lover who has walked out on you, or a boss who decided out of the blue that you no longer have a job. I will show you that you can achieve your full potential if you are willing to accept accountability for the way your life currently stands. Then – and only then – can you move forward.

There is No Such Thing as a Born Achiever

I believe that all of us were born with a healthy level of self-esteem. Can you imagine the nurses and doctors in the delivery room arguing over which kid is going to be a TV star and which kid a street sweeper; or which kid will be president of Australia (here's hoping!) and which kid will be a junkie? The bottom line is that we have all been given equal talents and equal levels of self-esteem. It's what happens *after* birth that will decide whether we run for The Lodge or run for another fix.

I am always struck by the startling differences between people who are travelling well in life and those who are not going so well. The people I am referring to as 'not going so well' are the ones who have every reason to be successful, but who are sitting around waiting for the lottery balls to drop in their favour so that everything will 'be all right'. What these people have not grasped is that they already have everything they need to become successful. All they need to do is start to expect more of themselves.

The Self-esteem Bank Account

Brian wrote to me after reading about the Self-esteem Bank Account in *You Can Do It!* He said that for years he had struggled with life in general and always felt that something was missing. When he read the chapter on self-esteem, he was shocked, and at the same time ecstatic, about what he had just learnt.

Your Self-esteem Bank Account operates just like your normal bank account, requiring deposits and withdrawals. When you do something good, you subconsciously deposit points into your Self-esteem Bank Account. But when you make a mistake, you subconsciously go to your Self-esteem Bank Account and withdraw from it. It's that simple.

Brian realised that when he was growing up, he had been scolded for saying anything positive about himself. His mother, who committed suicide when he was 12, never let anything positive be said in the house. For example, if Brian or his sister happened to say they'd done well in a test at school, they were told to stop big-noting themselves. You can imagine what effect this had on Brian's self-esteem. He said he couldn't believe how much it had affected him, but more importantly, he was staggered that while he knew his childhood had something to do with it, he had never realised the specific thing that was holding him back.

He said that the most amazing things have happened since he has started focusing on lifting his Self-esteem Bank Account – at 43 years of age. No longer is he giving away his power to his childhood – it happened, and that's that. Brian said that he had been to see many counsellors over the years, and they all had a version of why he had struggled for so long. Something as simple and basic as the Self-esteem Bank Account has finally provided him with a mental picture of what was happening in his head every time he berated himself for making a mistake.

Start to Focus on What You Want to Become

With so much strife throughout the world created by religious differences, it's amazing to discover that the different religions have so much in common. The major commonality is that the basis of their beliefs are prayers, chants and mantras. Now before you think I am getting on my high horse to start bible-bashing, reflect for a moment on why, throughout the ages, these basic beliefs have never changed. It's because, as human beings, we are built to be constantly moving forward – not so much physically as mentally in this case. All of these prayers, chants and mantras ask the person to look forward and have faith, and their lives will be better. I find it interesting that all of the major religions ask you to close your eyes and focus on what you want, not on what is currently going wrong in your life.

You will become whatever you focus on the most. But herein lies the biggest misconception about achieving health, wealth and happiness in your life. Many people believe that if they start to wish for the negative happenings in their life to cease, they will. Nothing could be further from the truth. If you start to focus on what you don't want to happen, you will eventually make it happen.

> We move towards, and become like,
> whatever it is we are thinking about most.

Rear-vision Thinking or Hands-on-the-steering-wheel Thinking?

It's pretty simple, really. If you are driving a car and keep your eyes on the rear-vision mirror, the chances of getting to your destination in one piece are remote. You would be hitting every obstacle placed in front of you, and blaming the obstacles for getting in your way and slowing you down – or worse still, making you stop in your tracks. The other option when you are driving is to grab the steering wheel, avoid the obstacles and drive to your destination.

Life works in the same way. Look back with regret and you are setting your life up for more setbacks; you will hit more obstacles. Grab the controls of your life and you will drive where you want to go.

One way of taking control is to change the way you speak to yourself and to others. Instead of making negative or 'rear-vision' comments, start using positive or 'steering-wheel' phrases. The more you use the positive comments, the more you will create a world where they will come to pass. In a way, you are 'pretending' that the positive outcomes have already happened.

Think about the flight simulator which pilots practise on at the jet base for months and months before they actually take off for an unfamiliar airport in another country. In the simulator, they see that airport and feel all its bumps and unique features just as if they were really landing with 350 passengers on board. This training is taken very seriously and everything is treated as if it's the real thing. Why? Because everyone in the airline industry knows the power of mental rehearsal and creative visualisation.

Here are some 'rear-vision' comments you might relate to, together with some 'steering-wheel' comments you could replace them with. If you cast your eye down the 'Steering-wheel Comments' below, you will notice that they are written in the first person, present tense. This is to help you program yourself with new information *as if it is already done.*

Just remember, the subconscious can't tell the difference between a real or an imagined event, so it is vitally important that you 'pretend' that the change has already been made.

Rear-vision Comments	Steering-wheel Comments
Relationships	
I will never trust a guy/girl again.	I have a loving and trusting relationship.
Girls/guys don't understand me.	I communicate my needs clearly.
I don't want to be lonely.	I'm okay with my own company.

Work environment

I hate this job. It stinks.	I am moving towards a successful career.
Everyone here is negative.	I inspire others to be positive.
I am not appreciated here.	Everyone respects my work ethic.

Health and wellbeing

I wish I could lose this flab.	I am moving towards health daily.
I am always running out of breath.	I am getting lighter and fitter.
Junk food is the only thing I have time for – I am always in a rush.	I only eat and drink food that will give me energy and health.
I am always getting sick.	I eat well and live well.
My back is killing me.	I now walk to provide flexibility.
I am sick and tired of my headaches.	I am now more relaxed every day.

Children and family

You will amount to nothing if you keep carrying on like that.	You're better than that, Mark.
That dress looks disgusting.	Hey Karen, what about that sexy blue dress you bought when we were at Surfers?
Your room's a pigsty.	Matthew, could you clean your room?

The way you look

I hate the way I look.	I radiate health and happiness.
My bum is too big.	I am moving towards a slimmer body.
I hate my breasts.	I love my body shape.
I wish I were pale/tanned.	My skin reflects a healthy lifestyle.

I hate school; it sux.	I am doing better every day.
This course is going nowhere.	This course is really happening.
I have never been good at XXX.	I am enjoying XXX more and more.

Your Crossbar of Achievement

Once you decide you want to become successful and work at it, you need to watch out for signs of complacency. If you achieve a certain amount of success and then sit back congratulating yourself, you will plateau out. Hundreds of people have heard me speak about this, and many of them have since told me that they realise they have plateaued out after they achieved some success in their life. Some got the promotion at work they always wanted, then lost all motivation and fell flat. Others won the qualifying race in their sport but failed in the major event.

Have you ever seen Australian pole vault champion Emma George in action? I am amazed at how this world-class athlete constantly pushes herself to new heights – literally. It seems that every week on the news we hear that she has broken another world record, pushing that crossbar higher and higher every time.

Now, while everyone knows that athletes must put in hours and hours of personal effort to achieve success, you might not be aware that the one element they have to have before anything begins is a belief that they *can* achieve a new world record, or that they *can* improve on their personal best.

Like sportspeople the world over, you must also question whether you really believe you can achieve your goals. You have set your own 'crossbar', and everything you are currently achieving has been 'cleared' by your self-image. Many people think that we evaluate an event *after* it has occurred, saying things to ourselves like,

'I *knew* I couldn't do it.' But the reality is that just as a pole vaulter knows before she jumps whether she is going to make it over or not, you too know *before* you 'jump' whether you will be successful. You have a conversation with yourself before the event as well, in which you query whether you can deal with the challenge ahead of you. Based on your evaluation, you are either successful or you fail. And this is where the 'I *knew* I couldn't do it' line kicks in.

You have set the crossbar of achievement in your life, and it's set tight. It's going to take courage and commitment to lift that crossbar higher. Always remember this major point: **first you have to believe, then you will achieve.**

Sales Targets are My 'Crossbar'

Damian is a home-loans consultant with Aussie Home Loans in Sydney. After attending my half-day seminar, Damian told me he had realised that while the company requires its loan consultants to achieve a certain personal level of sales, he had accepted the monthly sales targets from his manager without questioning whether he could do better. He has now decided that his sales targets – his personal 'crossbar' – are too low and that there is no reason why he couldn't add 10 per cent (or even 20 per cent) to that target, and achieve it.

Damian is like most salespeople, who accept their monthly targets as their 'crossbar' and strive to jump it each month. But, as Damian realised, you don't have to accept the limitations placed on you by your boss or company. Remember: the targets are formulated by the company to make the business profitable and successful, but no organisation ever had a rule which said you were not permitted to 'reset the crossbar of achievement'.

How My 'Crossbar' was Slipping Lower and Lower

Janine, a full-time mother of two toddlers, wrote to me about a recent incident in her life. She had attended a close school friend's shower tea, and after most people had left, she was having a cup of tea with two women who had stayed to clean up after the party. The day before, both women had attended one of my seminars, and Janine was impressed by what they said about it, especially the section on lifting your personal crossbar. Their discussion centred around how, when you get married, you start off with all the enthusiasm in the world, but how usually after a few years the passion starts to wane.

Janine wrote in her letter, 'I could relate to this a lot, because now that I'm at home with the kids full-time, I realised I have slowly let my personal "crossbar" slip. After I had my first child, I still visited the gym twice a week and made some good friends with other first-time mothers. But after the second child arrived, it was too easy to justify why I didn't have the time to go to the gym any more. Now I'm going twice a week. I've promised myself I will get back to the size I was before I had my first child. And I also got to thinking about what else in my life has plateaued out. What else have I got used to?'

You Set the Crossbar

Where in your life has your crossbar of achievement stayed too low? Like Damian, where have you let others set the height? Or like Janine, where have you simply lost focus and got used to the 'crossbar' slipping gradually? Have a good look at the areas in your life that you are currently feeling unhappy about. You might just find that the answer lies in lifting your personal crossbar of achievement.

Want to know more about...?

3

The buck starts here

All men dream but not equally.
There are those who dream at night
reaching into the dark recesses of their mind
to wake in the morning and to find it was vanity.

But the truly courageous are those who dream
during the day with their eyes wide open,
for they can make their dreams come true.

T.E. LAWRENCE

In this chapter:

- The difference between 'true accountability' and 'nice accountability'

- How your level of accountability determines how you rebound from setbacks

- Why telling other people your problems can limit you

- What are you putting up with that should stop *now*?

- Sonja's story – how to stand up for yourself when things aren't right

- Kevin's story – how self-sabotage can be your greatest enemy

- David's story – how he turned his family's attitude around

- No more excuses – you are in the pilot's seat of your life!

On a recent flight I was browsing through an Australian business magazine when I saw an advertisement for a leading financial services organisation. This line jumped out off the page to me:

If you don't win Lotto, what will you do?!

I thought the line was a terrific attention-getter, especially because for me it really hits the mark regarding the attitude of many people towards their life and their future. A lot of people think that one day their fairy godmother will touch them with a magic wand and all their problems – financial and other – will be solved. But as we all know, there is no such thing as a fairy godmother. The chances of such a being touching you in your lifetime are about the same as your chances of winning the lottery.

Will You Take 'Nice' Accountability or 'True' Accountability?

When you take true personal accountability for your life, you accept *total* accountability – not just what I call 'nice' accountability, but 'true' accountability. 'Nice' accountability is taking kudos for the things that are going well in your life but not taking the blame for things that are going badly. It's accepting that you are in the pilot's seat of your life only when everything is going 'nicely' – being cheerful only when everything is going well at school, at work or in the home. But as we all know, that is not how life works. Life doesn't always run to our schedule, and it's when you attract what you perceive as 'setbacks' in your life that 'true' accountability is tested.

Take 'True Accountability' and Let Go of the Past

If there is one thing I have learnt, it is that everyone on this planet has been tested, is being tested, or will be tested. Let me explain what I mean. Every single person is being challenged every day by setbacks and hardship. For reasons beyond our comprehension, some people get a little more hardship and some get a little less. But everyone is dealing with some sort of challenge. If you are to deal successfully with these 'setbacks', you need to take 'true accountability' – and this takes a lot of courage and willpower. It's easy to feel sorry for yourself and wallow in self-pity, but **by taking 'true accountability' for what's happened in your life, you can move forward with a sense of control**, knowing you are in the pilot's seat of your own life. When you hang on to the past, everyone around you treats you with pity. They treat you like a victim. In one sense, people get their kicks out of you reliving a past setback.

I experienced this phenomenon in the early days of my business. When I was struggling, and telling everyone about it, they would always ask after my business in a tone of voice which said, 'Loser! When are you going to wake up to yourself and give it away?' Then I changed tack and started 'feeding' them new, positive information. I was amazed to see how people's attitudes changed.

The shift in my thinking occurred during a visit to a bookshop. I don't remember where I was, but I do remember finding this quote.

> ## Don't tell a person your problem unless
> ## he or she is directly related to the solution.

Wow! Did these words give me a jolt, or what? I realised I had been telling anyone who would listen how badly my business was going, and expecting them to cheer me up.

This great advice was really rammed home when I went out to dinner soon afterwards with some family and friends. We were eating our entrees when my mobile phone rang. Normally I turn it off when I'm out to dinner, but I was waiting on this one call. I had told everyone there that I was expecting a new client to call to say yes to a fairly big contract.

Well, the call was my client, as expected, but the news was not what I wanted to hear. He advised me that he was not able to give me the go-ahead that night.

For ten years I have copped this sort of news, and like all salespeople, I have learnt to accept the punches and roll with them. However, this time it was different. Everyone on the table heard the conversation and gathered that I didn't get the contract. Now, I have had plenty of setbacks, but because I don't go around sharing them with everyone, people don't tend to remind me of my failures. I try to focus on where I want to go, and this is what I usually talk about when I meet family or friends. But for the next few months, whenever I saw anyone who had been at the restaurant that night, somehow, some way, they would bring up the lost contract.

The saying 'Don't tell a person your problem unless he or she is directly related to the solution' is one of the most powerful pieces of advice I have ever been given. From now on, why don't you make a decision to take 'true accountability' to let go of past traumas and replace them with a vision of where you want to go?

Silence is Consent

Wendy Matthews, one of Australia's best-known recording artists, has a great line in one of her songs, 'Friday's Child': 'If silence means consent'. This phrase always jumps out at me when I hear the song, because I believe that in many areas of our life we sit and take a lot of things we shouldn't put up with, instead of saying something. And by sitting there and not saying anything, we allow this bad situation to continue. We are not taking 'true accountability' for our own happiness, safety, or whatever else is being compromised.

Sonja's Story

Sonja realised how true this was at a seminar I gave for a leading car dealership. She told me afterwards that she had started to get upset with me when I started speaking about 'true accountability'. She had always thought that she took total accountability for her actions and couldn't see any area in her life where she was not doing this. But by the morning tea break, she had discovered one.

Sonja told me about one of her colleagues, who is always telling other people about the mistakes that happen in their department. In 99.9 per cent of the cases, the mistakes involve her and she comes out of each story looking like a clumsy no-hoper. She was upset by this, but had taken no action, preferring to think that no one would take much notice. Sonja said she could see now that because she had tolerated this behaviour by 'non-action', she was in fact condoning it – and so it continued.

She faxed me a few days later to say that after the seminar – which her colleague had also attended – she sat down with this person and laid her cards on the table. She told him exactly what was upsetting her and how she felt. She also made it very clear that she expected the behaviour to stop immediately. To her amazement, her colleague said that he had had no idea how distressed she had been. He went on to say that he had learnt a lot in my seminar too, and until then had not realised that his tale-telling was not only damaging Sonja's self-esteem, but taking away the power of their department by sharing its 'dirty laundry' in public.

I called into the dealership about two weeks later and caught up with Sonja. She looked like a different person. When I asked how things were going at work, she said that the episode described above was only the tip of the iceberg. After the situation at work began to improve, she had started noticing several other areas where she was allowing others to 'steer' her life, and where she could take more 'true accountability'.

Sonja told me she realised that from as long ago as her early schooldays she had always avoided confrontation. She would often arrive home from school upset after an incident of bullying or being 'picked on'. The next morning her mother would march up to the school to see the headmistress, insisting that she do something about the situation. Sonja now realised that because her mother had always 'taken over', she herself had never really learnt to cope with confrontation – which is a part of all our lives, whether we like it or not. Sonja said that even though she is now 36, she had been expecting her boss to solve her problems at work just as her mum had solved all her problems at school. Until she realised this, she had been angry with her boss for not stepping in to stop the tormenting at work.

Sonja now realises how much accountability she has been giving away to other people, notably her superiors (her boss and her parents). Recently she attended a conflict resolution class, which greatly assisted her both at home and at work. She told me, 'I no longer sit around wishing someone would stand up for me – now I stand up for myself. If there is a confrontation, I now approach it calmly but firmly and let the other person know that I won't be treated badly.'

And guess what? People are now responding to Sonja in a new, respectful way. They respect her because they sense that she respects herself enough to stick up for herself.

Where in your life are you accepting second-best? Where should you be speaking up and letting others know that you expect better treatment? Remember, if you set the rules, others will play by them!

Why Do I Keep Stuffing Up My Job?

Kevin, a salesman for a financial services company, told me he could relate to Sonja's story very easily. While he knew he was an exceptionally good salesperson, he never seemed to be able to hold down a job for longer than a few months. His moves were becoming so frequent that all his friends would 'jokingly' ask, 'Where are you working this week?'

Kevin said that he was in deep pain about the constant changes in his life – until he joined his current employer. In this job, as in his previous ones, his pattern was that whenever there was any sort of problem he would ignore it, hoping it would just go away. One day, one of his clients rang the boss to complain about Kevin's 'over-familiarity'. She said that he had become too 'pally' and that she wanted to deal with someone more professional. It wasn't the first time this sort of complaint had been made about Kevin. He was called into the boss's office to discuss his performance.

When his boss asked him to modify his behaviour, Kevin 'lost it'. He stood up and said that he was one of the higher-producing salespeople in the company, and if the boss didn't like his style he could sack him. But his boss knew that this was exactly what had happened at other places where Kevin had worked. Instead of dealing with the situation and learning from it, Kevin always chose to resign and never took 'true accountability' for what had happened.

This particular boss decided he would not take this. He said,

'Sit down!', then slammed the door shut and read Kevin the riot act, letting him know that the same thing had happened in every other company Kevin had worked in. Instead of aiming to become number one, he was satisfied with merely being in the top 20. He said Kevin could easily become a top-five producer within six months if he smoothed some of his 'rough edges'.

Kevin was dumbstruck – business can be pretty ruthless, and up to this point, whenever he had threatened to resign, his former bosses had always held out their hand, said 'Thank you' and accepted his resignation on the spot. Kevin said that in hindsight he could remember at least 20 accounts he had lost because he became too familiar with the client. He also realised that the reason for this problem was that he would start to doubt his own abilities and imagine the clients were 'going cold on his pitch'. Instead of solving the problem by improving his self-esteem and believing in himself, he ran away from it.

Kevin had just finished reading *You Can Do It!* and said that Chapter 10, 'The Teacher Arrives when the Student is Ready', was a powerful kick in the pants for him. He said that he could now see clearly how, by not taking 'true accountability' for his performance in every area, he was in fact asking the 'teacher' to revisit him until he got it right – in other words, until he learnt the lesson he was being taught!

Where in your life are you constantly being visited by a 'teacher'? In other words, where are you receiving constant setbacks? And how could you take more 'true accountability' to improve the situation?

I am Losing My Family and Friends

Have you ever heard the saying, 'It's lonely at the top'? David is the brother of the managing director of a corporation who booked me to do some seminars. He attended one of the seminars, and told me afterwards about an event in his life which had taught him, in a most powerful way, how failing to take accountability can cause havoc in your life.

For as long as he could remember, David had always wanted to renovate houses. He loved making things new again, and dreamt of one day owning his own design consultancy. His parents and family were not fussed about what he did, as they knew that whatever he chose, he would be good at it. David always felt they were on his side.

That was until he became successful.

David said that he had struggled for about five years to build his design business and had started to enjoy life immensely – with the exception of one area. When I asked him what area that was, he said, 'My family. As my success grew, my family started to become distant and aloof towards me.'

He went on: 'I didn't feel as if I had changed much, but I noticed that my family were becoming very negative every time I came into contact with them. I found myself not looking forward to visiting them, as every time I did, we would end up disagreeing about something.'

David said that he searched his mind for months about what he might have done to cause his family to act like this. The penny dropped when he was on a flight from Sydney to Perth. As the flight is of a decent duration, it provided a good chance to think without any interruptions. He realised that his family might be feeling threatened by his success. They were seeing constant reminders of David's upward mobility, such as flash cars and a new house, and were comparing themselves and their lack of achievement to him.

The first thing David did when he returned to Sydney was to sit down with each member of his family and ask them how they felt about his success. After initial comments like 'You know we are thrilled for you', each of them started to open up. They eventually got around to saying that they felt like they were losing him, that they could not keep up with his lifestyle and that they thought that *he* thought they were not important in his life any more.

David was shocked. How could they think that? He had never said anything to make them believe such a thing. After some more reflection, he realised that in order to take 'true accountability' for his own success he would have to bring things to a head and not let the issue fester away. He knew that if he left the situation as it was and continued to turn up at family events such as Christmas and Easter as if everything was okay, he would never be really happy. Any success he achieved would be a waste of time if he didn't have the love and support of his family.

What surprised him most was that his family members were in good jobs and doing well, and he had thought they were all very happy with their lot in life; yet as he started to dig deeper, he found that things were not as rosy as he had thought. He found out that his brother Dan's 15-year marriage was in trouble and Dan wasn't sure if David would be interested in listening to him and his problems. His sister Jill, who had been married for seven years, was trying to have a baby and was beside herself with frustration and self-doubt. Her marriage too was suffering. David was able to reassure Dan, Jill and the rest of his family that he still cared about them as much as ever and that they were an important part of his life.

He said, 'While my success is fantastic and my business goes from strength to strength, I feel much more at peace with myself now that I have cleared the air with my family.'

What he has done is take 'true accountability' for his life, to bring the problems to the surface and deal with them.

No More Excuses – I am in the Pilot's Seat of My Life

As you can see from Sonja's and David's stories, it takes a lot of courage to speak up when things are not going well. Sometimes – as in David's case – success brings with it new challenges, which have been sent to prepare you for what lies ahead. Kevin's story is inspirational because it demonstrates how easy it is to get locked into a 'cruising altitude' and then jump ship and run when things become too difficult. Life is going okay and you don't want to make waves in your life, so you keep on running – but the problem keeps following you.

Taking 'true accountability' for your life and all its challenges gives you a feeling of control, a feeling that you can learn from setbacks and then grow from them. In contrast, taking 'nice accountability' for your life sets you up for a life filled with unpredictability and pain. This is because the very events in your life that have been sent to assist you and to help you grow have been ignored.

Where in your life are you not 'in the pilot's seat'? Where are you not 'taking the controls' to solve challenges, and instead letting the problems fester and cause pain?

Take a moment right now to identify at least three areas in your life that are causing you pain, and decide now that you *do* have the solutions to these problems and you *can* stop that pain.

Most of all, remember that the buck starts here!

Want to know more about...?

4

Risk and fear – you've got to have a go

You can't jump a chasm in two small leaps!

ANONYMOUS

In this chapter:

- How your self-esteem determines how you see risk

- Changing your 'cruising altitude' to minimise risk

- Steven's story – how one man grew after his divorce

- How the same family produced one risk-taker and one risk-avoider

- John Symond's story – how he came back and started Aussie Home Loans

H

Have a go, mate! It sounds very Aussie, doesn't it? But it's good advice. You can't really hope to achieve anything substantial in life if you're not prepared to take a risk. There are very few successful people around, in any field of endeavour, who have not taken some risk or other. In fact, I read once that the amount of success you achieve in life is usually commensurate with the amount of risk you take!

How much risk have you allowed to flow into your life? How 'safe' is your current lifestyle? Where could you possibly enhance your life by stretching yourself a little bit further?

Risk and Self-esteem

The link between self-esteem and risk is undeniable. **No one takes a calculated risk without first believing that they will come through**. In other words, you have to believe in yourself before you take the plunge. How much you believe greatly affects how you view what happens to you.

The best way to understand risk is to bring it down to a basic level. Have you ever walked past a Santa in one of those large shopping malls? Have you seen those two-year-olds screaming at the tops of their voices when their mother goes to put them on

Santa's knee? When you're an adult, you know this is crazy, because you know Santa is there to bring presents and good things. But because really young children don't understand the concept of Santa just yet, they take one look and start to scream. What happens only 12 months later? With a bit more maturity (and after seeing hundreds of ads on TV!), children see Santa as a gentle, kind old man in a red suit who will give them presents, if they ask nicely.

We all have Santas we are scared of. Our cruising altitude (see Chapter 1) can hold us back from putting ourselves into successful relationships or positions that will enhance our life.

The bottom line is that all of us are presented with opportunities every day, which, because of our conditioning, we often reject. Instead, we elect to remain at our cruising altitude. But by doing this, we resist the chance to grow.

Changing the Cruising Altitude

To prepare for change, you have two choices. You can take a risk and throw yourself into the 'scary' challenge, or you can choose to change gradually. The gradual change is most people's preferred option, as it involves a minimum of discomfort and tension.

Being Scared at 40

Steve is a 40-year-old who has played football all his life. He used to think he was pretty tough compared to most guys his age. But his story is similar to many other stories I've heard.

When I first met Steve at a mutual friend's house, he was in the final stages of an amicable divorce. He told me there were no hard feelings in the break-up; it was just that he and his wife had 'grown apart'. After about a year had passed, I met him again at the same place, at a barbecue to celebrate our friend's 40th birthday. Steve and I got talking about how he had managed since his divorce. He told me he was amazed at how difficult he had found things.

He had had no problems finalising all the legal work, with both parties agreeing on who should have what. The most painful and frustrating part of the divorce had been learning to stand on his own two feet.

Steve said that until he was single again, he didn't realise how much he had been 'living in his comfort zone' and maintaining his 'cruising altitude'. He had found it quite hard to do things on his own. For example, eating out at a restaurant or going to the movies by himself had proved very difficult. For more than ten years he had always had the 'safety' of his wife by his side, and now he found himself struggling to feel comfortable doing basic everyday chores like the shopping. He had always thought that 'taking a risk' meant having the guts to put his body into a hard tackle or go bungee jumping or white-water rafting. That there could also be a 'risk' involved in day-to-day events, such as shopping at the supermarket, had never occurred to him.

Like Steve, we are all cruising at a certain altitude, and sometimes it takes a setback to really ram home how much we have plateaued out in life, how much we have let complacency set in. When was the last time you ate in a restaurant alone, or went to the beach or cinema by yourself? Try it this week and see how you feel. You might be surprised at what you discover!

Same Family, Different Altitude (and Attitude!)

Kenneth grew up in the same household as his older brother, Jim. They had the same parents and shared just about everything. They watched the same TV programs, went to see most movies together and holidayed together. Yet Kenneth is now a successful small-business owner, while Jim has been working in the same low-paid job for 15 years.

The one major difference in their lives is risk. Kenneth decided early on in his life that he wanted to 'have a go'; he wanted to work for himself one day. First he got a part-time job in the local electrical store during the school holidays. Working in his holidays was a 'risk' for Kenneth – he could have stayed at home, but instead he decided to go for it. Jim, on the other hand, just hung around the house during the holidays – in other words, he played it safe.

Kenneth left school and went straight to full-time work in the electrical store. The owner, Mr Wilkinson, was happy to hire him as a permanent as he was impressed with Kenneth's attitude to life and how he was always doing more than expected. Jim eventually found a job with a glass repairer. It didn't pay much, but Jim said, 'My big break will come, sooner or later.'

After working at the electrical store for more than two years, Kenneth decided he wanted more responsibility. He knew there was a risk that if he approached Mr Wilkinson with the idea of moving up the ladder, his boss might think he was being an upstart. The other choice was to stay in his job and not say a word – but then how would Mr Wilkinson know of his ambitions? He wasn't a mind-reader, after all.

So one afternoon, just after closing, Kenneth asked Mr Wilkinson if he could try working his way up to assistant store manager by this time next year. The boss was thrilled at Kenneth's initiative and agreed to let him try, but said that he would need to knuckle down and take more responsibility for the day-to-day operation of the store. The next 12 months flew by, and Kenneth duly became assistant store manager, just as he had planned. Over the next four years he worked his way further up, to store manager. He began to stand out among the employees at all the stores in the franchised group, being seen as a switched-on young guy – and a risk-taker!

Kenneth knew that if he could just keep on doing what he had done up to this point, he would advance through the franchise system just as quickly as he had climbed the ladder at his local store. But nothing prepared him for what lay ahead.

Kenneth Lands His Own Store

After attending a conference with Mr Wilkinson, Kenneth heard that there was a store being built in a nearby suburb which the company was looking to franchise out. Although he was still very young by business standards, Kenneth managed to arrange the finance to secure the deal. He received a brilliant reference from Mr Wilkinson, who was one of the most respected franchisees in Australia. In a matter of a few short years, Kenneth had risen from shop assistant to store owner. And all because he dared to take a risk – he dared to believe in himself.

Kenneth's brother, Jim, is still working at the glass company, still waiting for his big break to arrive. But as Kenneth knows, big breaks don't just 'arrive' – you create them.

'At Aussie, We'll Save You' – The John Symond Story

If ever there was an example of believe and achieve, here it is. It's the story of an Australian businessman who has revolutionised the home loan market in this country forever. Using those immortal words, 'At Aussie, we'll save you', John Symond has created an organisation of young, dynamic people who believe in his vision that every Australian not only deserves to have the opportunity to own their home, but should be able to buy it at some of the lowest rates in the world. Before Aussie came along, Australia's home loan interest rates were among the highest in the world.

So how did the son of immigrant fruit-shop owners living in country New South Wales achieve this enormous task? John's story is one of perseverance and 'never give up'. He found out first-hand what it was like to go from humble beginnings to great wealth and then to lose it all.

From Country Boy to Millionaire, Then Broke

Right from his earliest childhood, John knew he wanted to be successful. His family travelled from town to town and State to State looking for potential business opportunities, resulting in the young John attending 11 schools. But this was just one of the many challenges which eventually created one of Australia's leading business identities. The years ahead were to test John's mettle many times over before he would eventually achieve his dream.

In the late 1980s, he began to make a name for himself in the finance industry, which led to him creating a company called Mortgage Acceptance Corporation. The following years were golden. Not only was he enjoying the fruits of his efforts in setting up Mortgage Acceptance, he also got married. Things could not have looked much better. He had everything – he was the head of a successful corporation, his personal life was bliss and he was living in a luxury mansion on Sydney's North Shore and indulging his passion for expensive cars.

But as we all know, the late eighties held a nasty surprise for all businesses when the stock market crashed in 1987. This one single development played havoc with John's company, and after three years of struggle, he decided that enough was enough.

The ensuing years were sheer hell. Not only did he lose over $10 million of his own wealth, his personal life crumbled as well. With the tremendous stresses that occur in anyone's life when there is financial turmoil, John watched his ten-year marriage falter and then end in divorce. He was at his lowest point ever, finding out what life was like for many other Australians who, like him, were battling to stay afloat.

He was Being Prepared

John knew that this was the lowest of lows, but he also knew in his heart that it was happening for a reason – that he was being prepared for something greater. He could have done what many businessmen at the time did and just given up, or even ended his life. But John Symond is a fighter, and he knew that for his family, and more importantly for himself, he had to fight back.

During the next few years, he devoted 100 per cent of his efforts to repaying his creditors, eventually negotiating a deal with them that freed him up to focus on new opportunities instead of looking at past failures. Around this time, John heard about the interest-rate revolution in the United States, especially in the area of lending to first-home buyers. He could not resist the opportunity to find out more, and headed for a study trip abroad to see for himself what was happening in America.

Aussie Home Loans is Born

When he returned, John knew this was his big opportunity. At the time, Australia was burdened with outrageously high interest rates because of little or no competition between the major lenders – who happened to be the four biggest banks in Australia. Imagine how crazy it would have sounded if John had mentioned his plans to you over dinner. Here he is, at his lowest point financially, personally and emotionally, telling you he is going to take on the big banks on their home turf! Ridiculous! He's mad!

Well, John didn't think so, and in 1992, from a small rented office in Sydney's Parramatta, he created what was to become a revolution in the Australian finance industry – a revolution that would eventually see the Federal Treasurer stand up in Parliament and tell his fellow Aussies that if they weren't happy with their bank, they should shop around for a better deal, **and should consider Aussie Home Loans!**

Who would have believed that when John started Aussie Home Loans with only 12 staff, the company would eventually become a household name across Australia, employing 1000 staff and turning over nearly $7 billion in home loans to 90 000 Australians? In 1997 it made a profit of $8 million. And everywhere, Australians are reminded of John Symond's vision by those white four-wheel drive vehicles emblazoned with the Aussie Home Loans logo, making a clear statement about how different they are to the banks.

You Have to Believe You Can Come Back from Defeat

The John Symond story is proof that it's not how hard you get hit, but how quickly you get up that makes the difference in today's world. All of us are served setbacks, and no matter what your station in life, you *are* going to cop some. It's how you deal with these setbacks that will really determine whether you achieve more of your potential. John could easily have given up when the chips were down in 1990. When his marriage collapsed and all hope seemed lost, he could have decided that he had already had his fair share of success in life. He could have remained depressed about what had happened and what might have been.

John Symond is proof that we can all make a difference, but that the opportunity to achieve this difference might be presented to us in a most unlikely way. So have a look at some of the setbacks you have been given in the past, or maybe are experiencing right now. For John Symond, they were the opportunity of a lifetime – and maybe they are for you, too.

Want to know more about...?

5

The gift of setbacks

Only when it is dark enough can you see the stars.

RALPH WALDO EMERSON

In this chapter:

- ◆ Setbacks are a gift in disguise

- ◆ Tom's story – from cruel childhood to success

- ◆ Mark's story – how he lost $100 000 and then became a success

- ◆ The teacher arrives when the student is ready

- ◆ How a couple reinvented themselves after losing their income

- ◆ Overcoming a marriage breakdown and learning to trust again

In Chapter 3 you learnt how we are all being challenged every day by setbacks and hardship in our lives. In this chapter, I want to show you how these setbacks can be seen as valuable gifts. You're probably thinking, 'He's crazy! How can the words "gift" and "setback" be used in the same breath?' Yet I am convinced that each and every setback is preparing us for what lies ahead. Businesspeople, sports stars, Nobel Prize winners and others who have achieved success in their lives have experienced tremendous setbacks, yet they have prospered. Other less successful people just whinge about the hand life has dealt them. How come? Somewhere along the line the successful ones have learnt and understood that everyone is being prepared for what lies ahead by attracting setbacks. The setbacks teach us, strengthen us and, more than anything else, prepare us for new roles in life.

In *You Can Do It!* I shared how my life was thrown into turmoil with the death of my father when I was just 14 years of age. This trauma, while rocking me to my foundations at the time, was the single most important step for me in achieving success in my career. It prepared me for what lay ahead more than I could ever have imagined. I knew then that 'the buck started here'; I was not going to be given a free ride in life in any way. If I did not make things happen, myself, that was the end. I had to take total accountability to create happiness and success in my life – no excuses!

How Tom's Unhappy Childhood Propelled Him to Success

One of the fascinating parts of my job as a speaker and consultant is never knowing what a client or seminar attendee might tell me. The stories people share with me are always interesting and hold many lessons. But Tom's story was a bit closer to home than others. I could relate to him because we had both had setbacks in our early life.

Tom told me his story at the end of a seminar for a leading insurance company. He had had a terrible childhood and could still vividly remember hiding in a cupboard while his father went berserk during his daily drunken rampage. His mother was regularly bashed by his father, but did the best she could to shield Tom and his older brother, Brian, from harm. Despite her efforts, she could not screen out for them the awful sounds of the violence.

For Tom, life meant carrying on at school as if nothing was wrong at home. He told me that up until his twelfth birthday he thought every kid at school was bashed at home and all their mothers were treated in the same cruel manner as his dear mum. It wasn't till he was away on a school camp that Tom discovered that the other boys in his class looked up to and were mates with their fathers. This came as a huge shock, because up to this point he had never entertained the idea of being close to his father.

About a week after he returned from camp, Tom experienced yet another setback. His mother was hospitalised once again via the hand of his drunken father. She was supposed to be in hospital for two weeks but signed herself out a week early to look after her two boys. It was early evening when she arrived home. She noticed a light on in the bedroom and when she walked in she found her husband in bed with one of their neighbours. Tom and his mother and brother immediately moved out into a refuge. Later they moved interstate to make a new start and escape the hell they had endured all their lives.

Both Tom and his brother were subjected to this nightmare as children, but they chose different paths in their adult lives. Tom left school at the age of 15 and worked his way up the corporate ladder, eventually becoming state manager for a prominent insurance company. Brian, who left school at 18, went from one dead-end job to another, experimenting with drugs to deal with the pain of his childhood years. He is now dependent on heroin, and has been in trouble with the police on a number of occasions.

Tom had come to the realisation early on that **his childhood experiences could make or break him – and he knew the decision as to which was up to him**. He could either go off the rails or make a success of his life. He told me, 'I'm tougher than most. I chose to be a success.'

Tom has often seen his peers stressed out about little things, and can see that many of them don't know what real pain is. He said he could see my point about the 'setback as a gift' very clearly. While he would not wish his childhood on anyone, he now sees it as the 'one defining event' in his life which has made him a success today.

He Lost $100 000 . . . and Then Found Success

Mark, a successful financial advisor and speaker, is a terrific example of 'seeing setbacks as gifts'. He always wanted to be a speaker on financial matters, but didn't know how to get started on the speaking circuit. Then, in the late eighties, he heard about a British financial institution which wanted to be represented in Australia. The job entailed calling on Australian companies and selling them a video-based training package aimed at assisting their staff to better deal with their finances. Mark thought all his Christmases had come at once. This was the perfect opportunity to start his own business as a speaker. But as he was soon to find out, in a very traumatic way, this was also his greatest turning point, a 'setback as a gift'.

About six months into his business, Mark wasn't selling as many video packages as he had been led to believe he would. Companies were shying away from 'pommy' training systems and wanted systems with more Australian content. He was getting deeper and deeper into debt, and had added stress from the bank, who wanted his overdraft reduced. It was at $60 000 and Mark was getting really worried.

One of the few companies to hire his services was an Australian bank, who decided to give him a go and let him present at their annual convention in Hobart. During the presentation everything went smoothly until Mark asked the audience a question he always asked: 'What do you hate more than always running out of money?'

Someone answered, 'Watching pommy training videos.' Mark was really upset at this, but he didn't let on how affected he was and pushed on. Afterwards, everyone came up to him and congratulated him on his presentation except for the guy who had said he disliked British training tapes.

After lunch, everyone left to enjoy their free afternoon at the convention. Mark was in the lobby of the hotel preparing to check out when he felt a tap on his shoulder. To his surprise, it was the guy from the seminar. He introduced himself as Martin, and said that he wanted to apologise for causing any hurt to Mark by speaking up during the seminar and criticising the videos.

The 'setback as a gift' was right around the corner and Mark had no idea how this would change his life forever. The two men decided to sit down and discuss the financial markets and started to get on very well. Then Martin dropped the bombshell. 'Why the hell are you showing bloody imported videos which are outdated anyway? I was watching you and whenever you put on a video, you would lose the audience. But every time you personally summarised what the video had said, the audience came to life. Mark, what I am saying is: why don't you present the information live, in person, yourself? You have all the knowledge and experience, and most of all, you have the one ingredient that will make you successful – you have an Aussie accent.'

Mark couldn't believe what he had just heard. Martin was absolutely right. Five minutes ago he had thought this person was an enemy, but now he had turned out to be the biggest 'gift-giver' of all. Mark said it was like in a cartoon when the light bulb flicks on with the right idea. He knew from that moment that he was going to be a successful speaker. No doubts.

During the next three years, Mark pursued his career of speaking and struggled with a debt of now close to $100 000, but he didn't mind. He knew that very soon he would be earning higher fees, which would more than assist him to reduce his debt. Ten years on, Mark is a leading financial markets speaker. To this day, he says that his number-one turning point or 'setback as a gift' was when Martin spoke to him after that interruption during the seminar.

The Teacher Arrives When the Student is Ready

Mark is among the many readers of *You Can Do It!* who found the highlight of the book was the chapter called 'The teacher arrives when the student is ready'. I received hundreds of letters from people who expressed gratitude for learning this 2000-year-old Eastern quote, which enabled them to see clearly how past setbacks were now their greatest assets.

By seeing setbacks as your 'teacher', you start to achieve a new perspective. You choose to see incidents in your life not as accidents, but as events which prepare you for your future.

Beautiful One Day ...

Harvey is a great example of someone who experienced a kick in the guts and decided to make a choice between lying down and taking it, or getting up and fighting back. He attended one of my seminars on the Gold Coast and sat next to me at lunch. During the meal he told me how much he related to what I was saying. This time three years before, he had hit rock bottom. He had been working in Melbourne in a job he didn't particularly enjoy. The industry he was in was being affected by government tariff changes and becoming less economically viable by the day.

One very cold Friday afternoon, Harvey and his workmates were told that the factory was closing and they were all out of work – effective *now!* While shocked by the savagery of the announcement, Harvey had known it was inevitable and felt a sort of relief. When he went home to tell his wife, Jessica, she was also shocked, but relieved too – because she knew the writing was now on the wall. She and Harvey would both have to act, instead of waiting for a 'fairy godmother' to change their world.

After a week of settling their finances, Harvey and Jessica decided to move to the Gold Coast. The corridor between the Gold Coast and Brisbane is the largest growth area in Australia and they knew there would have to be jobs available for a hardworking couple. Jessica, who had stopped work five years earlier to look after their son, Ben, decided it was the perfect time for her to re-enter the workforce. An added incentive to move to the Gold Coast was that both Harvey and Jessica's parents had moved there to retire.

Soon after they moved, Harvey landed a job with a supermarket chain and Jessica accepted part-time work in a lawyer's office. Harvey said that while it had been a bit tough initially, settling in to the new environment, three years later they were just about to move into a new home which included a pool and water views.

He was recently promoted to supervisor, and Jessica had received a great boost when the partners in the law firm, impressed by her commitment to the firm and commonsense approach to solving problems in the office, asked if she would consider full-time employment.

Harvey told me: 'Many of my ex-workmates in Melbourne are still very bitter about what happened, and some are still unemployed. The biggest lesson I learnt was that when you take "true accountability" for your life you start to see options to make it happen. The only regret we have is that we waited so long for the Melbourne company to shut down – we should have made the change years ago, when we first talked about it!'

The Weekend that Changed a Life

Terry and Renee were going through a rough patch in their marriage. To get the spark back in their relationship, Terry decided to hire a houseboat for the weekend on Sydney's Pittwater. There is a really romantic atmosphere about watching the mist rise on an early Sunday morning in America's Bay – he had seen it before on fishing weekends with his mates, and decided he wanted to share it with Renee.

At first Renee resisted the idea, but eventually she agreed to go and everything was set. About a week before the event, Terry bumped into one of his former fishing mates, Gregory, and mentioned that he was going to be on Pittwater during the following weekend. He suggested that if Gregory was around he should call Terry on his mobile and they could meet up somewhere for lunch on the Sunday.

Terry and Renee looked forward to their weekend with great anticipation. Terry even noticed that as the weekend came closer, they stopped arguing and started to focus on what they were looking forward to.

It came around very quickly. The weather was perfect and the weekend was going terrifically well when Terry's mobile rang. It was Gregory, who had decided to take up Terry's offer to get together on Sunday for lunch. Gregory lived on Pittwater and had just bought a cruiser, so he would have no problem getting to the houseboat no matter where they were. They eventually met up at The Basin, a popular holiday spot only accessible by boat opposite Palm Beach.

Terry had thought Gregory would arrive with his wife, Stacey, and was surprised when he turned up alone. When Terry asked where Stacey was, he was shocked to learn that they had split up two years earlier and were now divorced. During lunch, he asked Gregory what had happened to end the marriage, and Gregory said that he and Stacey 'had just grown apart'. Terry knew what he meant.

After lunch, both boats headed back to Gregory's waterfront home, which was looking terrific. Gregory had achieved success in the stock market, got out when things were going gangbusters and then invested heavily in real estate. After selling many of his investments, he had bought this four-level mansion at a bargain price. Renee, clearly impressed, exclaimed, 'We would have to win the lottery to get into a house like this!'

On their way home, Terry and Renee started to argue about money and where they were going in life. What had been a great weekend was now ending as most of their evenings did – in a fight.

Six months passed and nothing improved. Terry was getting more and more stressed out with the situation. One Friday evening he got home from work and found a note from Renee on the dining-room table. She had left him. As he read the note, the full extent of the disaster hit him. Renee said she had decided to move in with Gregory and that the lawyers would be contacting him soon to work out their separation and divorce.

The following two years were hell for Terry. He became bitter and angry towards Renee and his former 'mate', his health began to deteriorate and his weight started to increase. He was particularly depressed at Christmas. Every other year he had always done something with Renee and her friends, but the Christmas after the divorce, he spent the whole day watching TV.

A Christmas to Remember

By the next Christmas, Terry had come to realise that as long as he maintained his anger towards Renee and Gregory, his world would reflect that anger. He resolved to change his attitude.

As part of his new outlook, Terry decided to visit a hospital on Christmas Day and try to cheer up any patients who were alone. When the day came, he had a terrific time. The patients seemed to enjoy talking to him and he liked meeting them and hearing their stories. When he was in the cancer ward, he noticed a nurse adjusting an intravenous drip. He introduced himself and found out that her name was Belinda.

Later, when visiting hours were coming to a close, he decided to call it a day and go and have lunch. Just as he was leaving, Belinda came back into the ward and wished all the patients a merry Christmas. Terry – who is not normally backward in coming forward – asked her if she was joining her family for lunch. She replied that all her family lived in Cairns, and she was going home to her cat and dog. Terry seized the moment and asked her if she would like to come and have Christmas lunch with him at Darling Harbour. She accepted – and as they say in the classics, the rest is history. Six years later, Terry is happily married to Belinda and they have four kids!

Terry wrote to tell me his story after he read *You Can Do It!* He particularly identified with the chapter on setbacks, and said, 'I realised that the bottom line in life was to take total accountability for what happens and not pass the buck, no matter how bad it gets. If I had gone on stewing over my marriage break-up, I would have gone bananas. One of the reasons why my marriage with Renee broke down was because I wasn't good at sharing my feelings. Instead of discussing problems as they arose, I used to bottle up my anger or displeasure and eventually overreact to some little thing weeks later.'

When Terry made that decision to stop showing his anger to the world, it started reflecting his new attitude and he was able to move on. He said he has never felt better in his life, ever – and he repeated 'ever'. His final words were, 'Setbacks are definitely gifts in disguise. My four kids and fantastic wife are proof that we are all being prepared for what's coming down the track.'

We all know that setbacks can be painful, because we have all experienced them. In the end, I believe that the amount of success you achieve in your life is determined by one thing: deciding that setbacks are preparing you for the future instead of deciding to be a victim of them. You are the only person who can decide this. Setbacks *will* crop up in your life, and the way you decide to react to them will go a large way towards determining your future.

Like Terry, many of my readers have written to me describing how they have overcome adversity to find success and happiness. Their stories are proof that we can all come back from setbacks – if only we make that commitment to ourselves to believe that setbacks truly are a gift.

Want to know more about...?

6

Who said so?

The only ceiling in life is the one you give it.

ANONYMOUS

In this chapter:

- Kicking the pedestal – why you must challenge some of your parents' beliefs

- Your beliefs about money and your upbringing

- Who is programming your thoughts now?

- How looks really are irrelevant – it's what's on the inside that counts

- Real men *do* cry – what a relief

- It's okay being single!

- Mid-life crisis and what causes it

- Why you have to look after your own dreams in a relationship

- A parable for today – another angle on 'Who said so?'

- How teenagers can manipulate parents

H ave you ever had a good look at some of the beliefs you collected while growing up? These beliefs have conditioned you to respond to things in a certain way, and your responses have then led to certain choices. A lot of people are unaware of why they respond to things the way they do, and make their choices without thinking. The problem is that these choices may not be the right ones to make in order to achieve success.

I can hear you asking, 'How can you make a choice without thinking about it first?' Simple. Unless you sit down and have a good hard look at how you respond to certain circumstances, you will continue to respond 'unconsciously' to those situations the same way you always have, no matter how inappropriate your response might be.

Time to Kick the Pedestal

I don't mean this in a disrespectful way, but I am amazed at how many people still think their parents know best. They might have known best while you were growing up, but that's because they were the most important adults in your life at that time. Think about it for a moment. At school, you looked up to your teachers; at home, your parents were your guiding lights. They brought you into this world, fed you and financed you until you were old enough to support yourself, and for all that you are truly grateful. But now that you are an adult yourself, their beliefs are not necessarily your beliefs. You may still have some of their outdated beliefs, which are holding you back from achieving success in various areas of your life.

The reality is that if you do what your parents did, you will end up just like them. If that's what you want, great. But many people want to move on and achieve different things to their parents. Wanting to do that doesn't mean you're being ungrateful to them; it just means that you might have to break down some of the old-fashioned beliefs you have in your head.

Spring-clean Your Belief System

Rachael is a good case in point. She wrote to me expressing how much she had enjoyed reading *You Can Do It!* For years she had wanted to pursue further education, but every time she came close to signing up for a course, her parents would start to complain how much they needed her at home and how they wouldn't cope if she wasn't around. Eventually she came to see this for what it really was – emotional blackmail – and decided that if she was really going to be true to herself, she would sign up and start her new quest for education whether her parents liked it or not. After all, she was 28 years old!

Once she had made this decision, Rachael said, the most amazing thing happened. As soon as her parents realised she wasn't going to change her mind, they began to support her. What she saw, loud and clear, was that her ethnic parents' conditioning was restricting her from achieving her full potential. 'My parents' upbringing had taught them that the men in the family were the providers and the women's role was basically to look after the men.'

Rachael's desire to further her education was contrary to these beliefs, but perfectly in keeping with modern Australian society. She said, 'Mum and Dad weren't going to change their habits of a life-time overnight, so I knew I had to be strong and stick to what I believed was the right thing for me. But as soon as I challenged some of those old beliefs, my parents followed in support.'

Rachael now knows that there are many instances in her life where she has given away her personal power to her parents, because she 'thought they knew best'. As she said, 'They came to Australia without being able to speak a word of English and did a marvellous job raising five kids, and we're all now doing extremely well in our chosen careers. But now it's time for me and my brothers and sisters to start showing some leadership at home.'

Rachael finished her letter by telling me that, strangely, her parents are now eagerly waiting for more surprises from her!

How Do You Feel About Money?

During a consulting session with one of my clients, the subject of money came up. We were talking about our childhood conditioning towards money and how it had affected us as adults. My client, John, told me he had become wealthy because he *did not* listen to his parents' advice.

I said, 'Did you say you *did not* listen to them?'

He replied, 'Exactly. I love my parents and would do anything for them, but when it comes to handling money, they have no idea. They have struggled all their life, and even now, when they are in their sixties, they are still living in a very basic manner. I realised very early on that if I took their advice about money, I would prob-ably end up like them in this area of my life – and I didn't want that. When it came to morals and ethics, I could find no better teachers than Mum and Dad, but handling financial matters isn't one of their strong points.'

In many of my seminars I have had people come up to me and tell me they have realised, like John, that they were conditioned at home to be very wary towards money. Sue Ellen, a property consultant, said she had been working since she was 15 and had saved some money, but found it amazing how, every time she reached a certain amount in her bank account, alarm bells would start to ring and she would hear her mind saying, 'Spend it! Spend it!'

She said that after having a good think, she had traced this attitude back to her childhood. Her parents had only just managed to 'get by' when she was young, and she remembers vividly that every time her father returned from a cross-country job with his pay packet, her mother would loosen the purse strings and go on a spending spree. Two weeks later she would be saying, 'We have no money to spend. We have to tighten our belts.'

Who is Programming Your Thoughts?

It's quite funny when you come to think of it. Fashion dictates what's in and what's out for the coming year. Are large sunglasses in, or will you be wearing those small, killer loops this summer? Are high heels in, or is it platforms? Is it long hair, or a number one? All of us are in some way questioning what we are wearing, eating, driving or watching via 'what's hot and what's not'.

The Slimmers' Disease – Both Women and Men Suffer

Pick up any magazine today and you will see the messages screaming out at you. They won't say it in so many words, but they are all telling you how slim you should be, what colour your hair should be, what colours are 'hot' in clothes, what breast size women should possess, how macho large biceps are on men, and so on and so on. We might all scoff at these magazines, but their portrayal of 'beautiful people' is pretty hard to resist.

I am always moved when I see those segments on TV current affairs shows about people with the eating disorders bulimia and anorexia nervosa. No one quite knows what causes these tragic conditions, but most people agree that the portrayal of women in glossy magazines has a fair bit to do with them.

And what about those 'over-the-top' male body-builders you see around? Some of these guys have fantastic bodies which create envy among their mates. But in the same way as the slimmer 'knows' that if she misses just one more meal she will attain the 'perfect' slender body, the body-builder looks forward to 'one more' set of weight-training, after which he will finally attain 'Mr Universe' looks. In some ways, body-building is like a male 'slimmers' disease'.

The sad connection between these conditions is that at the heart of both of them is a lack of self-love or self-esteem. **When you truly love yourself, you get a voice inside that says, 'I'm okay just as I am.'**

Next time you find yourself thinking, 'I'm too fat' or 'My body is pathetic', ask yourself these questions. Who am I listening to? Who says they are right?

I am a Tough Guy – I Think!

At a seminar I was giving for a major phone company, a guy called Nathan asked if he could have a chat with me. As soon as I met him, I had an idea what he might want to talk about. You see, Nathan was very obviously a body-builder who had spent many hours in the gym striving for peak fitness.

After the seminar was over, I met up with him and we discussed the contents of the seminar. Nathan said he was really amazed to hear me talk about the link between body-building and self-esteem. He told me that during his school years he had seen himself as a 'quiet achiever'. He went on: 'I wasn't a star pupil, but at the same time, I never really hit it off with girls like my mates did. I put this down to my lack of muscles, so when a neighbour suggested one afternoon that I come to the local gym, I decided I had nothing to lose. As soon as I walked into the gym I was hooked. There were all these well-built guys around my age, and I decided instantly to turn my physique around and work towards looking like them.'

Five years after walking into that gym, Nathan has a body most guys only dream about. Yet he is still struggling to find a partner. After the seminar, he realised that the reason for this was how he sees himself on the inside – it's not because there's anything wrong with how he looks on the outside.

About three months after our meeting, I received a phone call from a very excited and positive Nathan. He said, 'I feel like I've finally found the missing jigsaw piece. I've decided I'm going to build myself up in terms of self-esteem the same way I built myself up physically. Who knows what will happen from here? I'm very optimistic!'

A Mother's Anguish

Shirley is a mum with four kids whom she loves very dearly. She wrote to me after she read *You Can Do It!*, saying she had passed the book on to her daughter Kate, who she believed could be in the early stages of bulimia.

Shirley said that while there was nothing specific in the book about bulimia, she had instantly thought of Kate when she read the chapter on self-confidence. She had watched Kate go through her teenage years with a lot of difficulty compared to her brothers and sister. Her panic attacks and bulimic-type behaviour began in Year 12. At first they happened only occasionally, but as the year progressed and the pressure mounted, Kate grew more and more 'into herself'. Shirley realised that the disorder or disease was more complex than she had first thought, and persuaded Kate to receive treatment at a local clinic, to prevent her from advancing to full-blown bulimia. Shirley said she and her husband were planning to do everything they could to keep Kate's self-esteem up, as they now understood that low self-esteem was one of the contributors to this debilitating and tragic condition.

Who Said Real Men Don't Cry?

Another belief that can be very harmful is the one that says 'Real men don't cry'. If you have been given this belief at some time in your upbringing, you'd better get rid of it straight away! All Eastern religions – some of which date back 2000 years or more – promote the value of having quiet time with yourself to get in touch with your feelings. I believe that when we feel sad or depressed, there is a message trying to come out, and that we should encourage this, not smother it.

I'm not saying you have to burst out crying every time something doesn't go your way, but when you're feeling down or just 'sick of life', try this. Go and have a good cry in your bedroom – just like you did when you were a kid – and watch how much better you feel afterwards. Crying is just as much a part of life as laughing, so the next time you feel 'blue', let your body bring you back to wellbeing with a good cry. If your conditioning has been such that you can't get your tears to flow easily, hire a tearjerker video – it should help!

Who Said You Can't be Happy being Single?

Travelling has always been a part of my life – first when I was in the travel industry and flying overseas on a weekly basis, and more recently, travelling interstate every week as a professional speaker and consultant. I love the freedom travel provides and the constant excitement of never knowing what's around the corner. Small annoyances, like flight delays, weather closing in and 'the passenger from hell' sitting next to you, only add to the excitement. So it comes as quite a surprise when I hear people constantly saying how they are 'looking for Mr or Ms Right', that their life is nothing without someone special and that they doubt they will ever find the person of their dreams.

In those times of my life when I've been single, I've found it a cathartic experience to walk into a restaurant by myself and have dinner. When I'm interstate, I enjoy sitting by myself in a café for breakfast rather than getting room service.

I can't tell you how many people have come up to me at the end of a seminar and said, 'It would be a lot easier to embrace some of your concepts if I was single.' Or, 'If only I could find someone to work through the changes with, it would be so much easier.' These are crazy things to say! **If you want to change your life, *you* have to make it happen**. Having a partner makes no difference.

Mid-life Crisis is Caused by Not Listening to Yourself

Have a look at your average Australian guy. He will usually go from living with his parents to moving in with his girlfriend – from his mother's apron strings to his girlfriend's. The situation with most women is similar. They go from their parents' 'safety house' to the 'safe house' of the man of their dreams. Then, after looking after the kids and the home for ten years, they have a good look at themselves and ask, 'What have I really achieved?'

The bottom line in most marriages, as I see it, is that the woman carries the load at home – even if she works – because her man has never really grown up. He has never had time to live by himself and discover who he is. When the man and woman are both nearing the age of 40, they start to question their lot in life.

I once read that the cycle of questioning happens every seven years from the day you are born. This means that you take a good hard look at yourself about every seven years and ask, 'What's life all about?' and 'Where am I going?' For me, the biggest events in my life have happened at these intervals. My father died when I was 14, which was when I decided to take total accountability for my life. At 21, I landed the job of jobs in the travel industry. Then, when I turned 28, I decided to start my own business and commence speaking professionally. And at 35, I landed the book deal with Penguin.

From all the consulting I have done and the thousands of people I have met at my seminars, I have learnt that if you don't listen to yourself at these times of 'questioning', you set yourself up for a barrage of turmoil at the next interval. That's why I think we bring the ubiquitous mid-life crisis on ourselves. I believe mid-life crisis happens when you have ignored the questions which have popped into your mind during the past intervals, that is, at the ages of about 14, 21, 28 and 35. When you near the age of 42 the circuit becomes overloaded, and the circuit-breaker says, 'Hold on! I want answers now!'

And because the questions are popping up every day at an amazing rate, everything is turned upside down in your life. This is the period when men buy a red sports car or trade their wife in on a young woman who knows nothing about life. Women at this stage of life often become severely depressed at where their life is at.

Relationships are a Two-way Street

Ross attended one of my seminars and told me he was stunned when I started talking about the seven-year cycle, because he had seen it happening in his own life. He said, 'I went straight from my mum's apron strings to being married, but thought nothing of it until your talk. At the moment my marriage is at an all-time low, and now I know why. In 15 years of marriage I've seen some great opportunities come along, but I've always passed on them because my relationship had to come first. I've had quite a few reservations about our marriage over the years, and I can see now that my wife, Penny, who is pretty strong-willed, was just a replacement for my mother. I've been really upset with myself for not going after my dreams, and I've been taking it out on our relationship.'

When I asked Ross what he would say to others in his situation, he replied, 'Relationships are a two-way street. You need to consider the other person, but you also need to look after your own dreams and goals. If you don't, you risk ending up bitter and twisted and resentful to the other person for holding you back. It all comes out eventually, usually when you're having a fight.'

Whereabouts have you given away your personal power to someone without considering your own needs and wants? Have you had setbacks at or around the points of the seven-year cycle? Did you look on these setbacks as turning points for future growth? Finally, have a good look at any outdated beliefs you might have inherited from your parents or brothers and sisters and start to replace them with new beliefs which better suit who you are today.

'Who Said So?' Also Applies to Kids

Up to this point, I have discussed how the beliefs given to you when you were growing up could be affecting you now. But what about the beliefs that parents get from their kids? Is it possible that parents can be conditioned by their kids? Well, I can share with you many stories of people in their fifties who are being held back by their teenage and twentysomething kids – and many of them don't even realise it.

Sounds crazy, doesn't it? Why would parents, fully grown adults, feel constrained by their kids? Surely they would just put the kids in their place and tell them to do what they are told. But as we all find out in life, some days and years are good ones and some days and years are sent to challenge us. When you are in the middle of one of those years when nothing seems to be going right for you, it's very easy to be swayed by the people close to you. For parents, teenage and twentysomething kids can be pillars of strength during a crisis, but they can also be very manipulative.

The following story was given to me more than 12 years ago by a business acquaintance. It really struck a chord with me because I believe we are all being 'programmed' daily by people around us (both adults and kids), the media (both electronic and paper) and the millions of advertising signals we see and hear.

This story clearly demonstrates the Henry David Thoreau quote, 'Once a seed is planted, it never shrinks – it just grows.'

A Parable for Today

A man lived by the side of the road and sold hot dogs.
He was hard of hearing so he had no radio.
He had trouble with his eyes so he read no newspapers.
But he sold good hot dogs.
He put up a sign on the highway telling how good they were.
He stood by the side of the road and cried, 'Buy a hot dog, mister.'
And people bought.
He increased his meat and roll orders.
He bought a bigger stove to take care of his trade.
He made enough money to send his son to university.
But then something happened . . .
His son came home from university to help him run the expanded business.
His son said, 'Father, haven't you been listening to the radio?
Haven't you been reading the papers?
If money stays "tight", we are bound to have bad business.
There may be a big depression coming on.
You had better prepare for poor trade.'
Whereupon the father thought, 'Well, my son has gone to university.
He reads the papers and listens to the radio,
and he ought to know.'
So the father cut down on his meat and roll orders,
took down his advertising signs,
And no longer bothered to stand on the highway to sell hot dogs.
And his hot dog sales fell almost overnight.

Elaine Breaks Free of Her Kids

Elaine attended one of my seminars in Melbourne. She was a single parent in her early fifties whose husband had been killed in a car crash seven years before. Elaine had recently thought it was time she let her hair down a bit. She wanted to meet other people her age with whom she could attend social functions and generally enjoy life a bit more.

But as soon as Elaine mentioned this idea to her two kids, both of whom were in their twenties, she copped pressure and 'stirring' from them about it all being due to the mid-life crisis. She was very hurt – all she wanted was to go out a few nights a week! Elaine said she realised then how much she had been subtly conditioned by her kids to stay at home and look after their needs while sacrificing her own. She had never thought that she could be so influenced by her kids. They were always asking her, 'Mum, can you do this' and 'Mum, can you do that'.

Elaine said, 'The reality is that they are too dependent on me, and it's about time they started doing a few things around the house themselves. Ever since my husband died, I have felt guilty about the kids not having a father, and I've been wrapping them in cotton wool. From now on I'm going to pay a lot more attention to *why* they say things, instead of just operating on ''autopilot'' and doing what they ask.'

Want to know more about...?

7

What's good enough for you?

Hold yourself responsible for a higher standard than anybody else expects of you.

HENRY WARD BEECHER

In this chapter:

- ◆ How your expectations have expanded and grown over the years

- ◆ Where are you accepting second-best in your life?

- ◆ Why do you give your guests better treatment than yourself?

- ◆ How appearances do matter and how to improve them

- ◆ How debt and goals are linked

- ◆ No one can give you love

- ◆ Self-love – the greatest love of all

W e all have proof of how much we have grown. For example, we have photos of past Christmases and birthdays, where we might be horrified at our former dress sense. Having that photo also brings a sigh of relief that we don't look like that any more (or wear those flares any more!). Like photographic proof of how you have changed over the years, there is also proof around you of how far you have come in a financial and physical sense.

Revisiting a Former Home

If you want to see how far you have come in your thinking regarding what's good enough for you, try to visit a house you used to know well – maybe the family home you grew up in, or your grandparents' home. Watch what happens when you walk in after all these years. What is the first thing you notice? Of course – everything has shrunk! Everything has got smaller.

The first apartment I lived in after I moved out of my family home was a nice little one-bedroom place in Neutral Bay, on Sydney's lower North Shore, overlooking the city skyline. I decided one day recently to call in and see who lived there now. When I knocked on the door, a man of about 40 opened it. I was wearing my suit, so who knows what he was thinking! Very quickly, I told him who I was. I had brought some registration papers with the old address on it so he could see I was genuine. After a bit of hesitation, he said, 'No problem,' and let me in.

I couldn't believe how small the apartment was. The ceiling was so low it felt like things were on top of each other. And the noise! The place was located right next to the Warringah Expressway leading onto the Harbour Bridge. I couldn't believe I had lived here for more than two years and enjoyed every minute of it. It was a massive reminder to me how we can accept anything in our lives, how we can get used to anything.

The most amazing thing is this: we can also achieve a lot more than we are currently achieving. What have you got used to which could be limiting you? What have you got used to which could be limiting your income, your family or even your health?

What are You Putting Up With?

Did you know that survey after survey has shown that at a restaurant most people will not complain if something is wrong with their meal? They will just sit there and eat it, or worse still, leave it. And then, without any hint of dissatisfaction, they will pay the bill. These surveys have also confirmed that such customers will most likely not come back to that restaurant again.

But this chapter is not about customer service. It's about making some tough decisions about what is good enough for you. I'm not for one moment suggesting you should create a scene when something doesn't go your way in a restaurant. What I am asking you to do is to have a good look at what you are putting up with in all areas of your life.

In my job I get to meet top achievers every day in every field. One obvious trait in high achievers is that they are never happy with the status quo, with the way things are. They are always questioning what could be, and if they can't see it, they set about creating it. They don't just do this in their working environment, but seek to achieve it in all facets of their life. Hence their personal growth is faster than most because they are always aware that it's their thinking, more than anything else, that will decide how much they eventually achieve in life.

How much have you challenged your current state of events? How much change have you introduced into your life in the last couple of years? To really achieve your full potential, you must strive to introduce new adventures and experiences into your life.

We Have Guests Coming – We'd Better Clean Up

Does it strike you as odd that most people, when they have guests coming over for dinner (or worse still, staying the night!), run around like a chook with its head cut off? Every other day they put up with the bathroom looking grubby or their bedroom looking like a bomb has hit it – but as soon as guests are expected, everything changes.

When you think about it, this is a pretty strange attitude to have. From now on, I want you to start treating yourself like your own very special guest. Pretend that for the next two weeks you have a very special guest staying with you. What changes will you make? How clean will the kitchen be? How tidy will the garden be? How many times will you disinfect the toilet with one of those nice deodorisers?

You get my drift, don't you? You are more important than any guest, so from today onwards, start to keep your surroundings in first-class style, as if you had the boss coming over for dinner, or even staying with you for a week! Just as you became used to leaving the bed unmade and the bathroom in a mess, you can become used to making your bed every morning and cleaning as you go.

I believe that the way you keep your home, your car and even your clothes is basically a reflection of your self-esteem, determined by what you think is good enough for you. Once you start to expect a higher standard in one area of your life, you will automatically start to lift the crossbar in other areas.

Dress as if You Will Appear on the Front Cover Today

I remember reading a magazine article about six years ago on 'dressing for success'. It was about which clothes make the best impression in the business world, what colours are 'in', and so on. Of all the information this article provided, one item jumped out at me and really hit home.

The point that made such an impact was one which said you should always leave home as if you were going to appear on the front page of your major newspaper. 'Wow!' I thought. Every business day I would try to put my best foot forward when it came to dress standards, but I realised I was letting myself slip up during the weekend. I used never to shave on weekends unless I was going out in the evening or working, but after I read that article, I decided to begin to shave every morning without fail. Since I started doing this, I have bumped into many clients and seminar attendees during the weekend at shopping malls, cinemas and restaurants, and every time I do, I thank my lucky stars that I read it, because I now realise what could have happened if they had seen me not looking as well presented as they remembered me.

If my clients have come to expect me to dress superbly at work, and they saw me looking like a slouch on the weekend, they might start to think, 'He isn't very consistent – what will he be like a year from now, when we are into our contract with him?' The old saying **'An ounce of image is worth a ton of performance'** is so powerful, yet many of us only apply it to working hours. The message of inconsistency is the last thing I want my clients to receive about me – so I have sharpened my game and try to dress appropriately and professionally no matter where I go. You never know who you are going to bump into!

A big point needs to be made here: **who says you can't relax when you are clean-shaven and dressed immaculately?**

Think back to when you attended a special friend's wedding or a school formal. How did you feel when you were getting dressed? Did your feelings about yourself improve? What happened when you were all done, and took one final look in the mirror to make sure everything was right? I'm sure you felt very pleased with yourself and started to look forward to the event with great anticipation.

Life is no different. If you can dress up a bit more, you will start to feel better about yourself. Not only will you feel better on the day (or night!), but you will set your self-talk off in a positive new direction as others start to compliment you on your smart new look. Keep it going every day and watch what happens. You might just be surprised at how much difference it really makes.

Expanding Your Expectations

One of the most telling signs of your conditioning and current belief system towards prosperity and abundance is your reaction to other people's success.

Growing up in Sydney's western suburbs, living above a grocery store, I always had dreams of living in a big house one day with views and a large driveway. One of the first things I did when I got my drivers' licence was to drive over the Sydney Harbour Bridge to the North Shore and northern beaches and have a look around the exclusive suburbs that nestle along the waterfront. I looked at the manicured lawns and immaculate driveways with their large iron gates, and was mesmerised by the sheer size of each house and the high standards with which they were maintained. Every time I visited these suburbs I felt great. I knew this was where I would live one day.

One spring afternoon I decided to drive to the northern beaches and have lunch at Palm Beach. As I had done on many occasions before, I drove around some of the most beautiful streets in Australia, all with fantastic views of Pittwater and the Pacific Ocean.

Then something strange happened. I saw an 'Open for Inspection' sign in front of a large, rambling house, and decided to stop and have a look around. I don't know what the sales guy thought of me, but I said to myself, 'Who cares? He can't stop me.'

When I saw the place, my eyes opened wide and I was dumbstruck. The boy from the western suburbs had never seen a house this large, which seemed to have everything – a tennis court, a swimming pool, a massive kitchen and a dining and living area bigger than the home I was living in! I had read many self-help books by this stage and knew that the basis for achieving anything in your life was first to believe it could happen, that once you could 'feel the achievement' you were halfway there. Something happened that afternoon which has lived with me ever since. Literally on the spot, I felt my beliefs towards wealth change. I could hear my self-talk accepting this as my new standard and convincing me that this was where I would live one day.

Aim Higher and You Will Achieve

Ever since that 'house inspection' I have tried to emotionally prepare myself for events that are coming down the track. When it comes to setting goals, I am always amazed that as soon as I commit to setting a higher standard, I start accepting that I can do it. I have noticed this in many areas of my life. For instance, as soon as I commit to buying a certain type of car, and spend endless sleepless nights wondering whether I will be able to pay for it, it's only a matter of months after the purchase that my 'cruising altitude' is set and I am thinking about my next car – what make it will be and how much I will spend.

If you can vividly imagine what you want, you will start to bring about events in your life to make it a reality. You can read more on mental rehearsal in Chapter 10.

Get into Debt – and the Money Will Come

If you ask your friends how to get the material things you want, most of them will tell you that you first have to save the money and then you will be able to buy it. But did you know that the way wealthy people become wealthy is to use debt to their advantage? They know that once they have set a goal – any goal – they start to see how to achieve it. As Henry David Thoreau said, 'Once a seed is planted, it never shrinks – it just grows.'

One of Australia's wealthiest men once told me that the way to attract wealth into your life is to get into debt. He said that when everything is going okay, you not only plateau out in your mental motivation, but you lose the drive to earn more. He said that when you know you have to earn a certain amount a month to meet your debts, you get cracking to do so.

Think of your first home mortgage and the worry you went through about whether you were going to make each repayment on time. Would you have enough cash each month to service the debt? Years later, you find yourself not only easily repaying the debt, but thinking of doing some renovations!

Whereabouts in your life have you let yourself slip? For example, how long have you had your current car for? If you want a new car, this is a great incentive to knuckle down at work and earn a pay rise.

Now if you're thinking, 'Hey, I will get the pay rise, then I will get the car', *no no no*. **The goal comes first and *then* you see how to achieve it**. Commit to a deadline and stick to it and watch what happens with your attitude at work. When you know you have that snazzy new car arriving in three weeks, you will start to find ways to earn more. Your other choice is to stay with the car you currently drive and keep on complaining that you never get any lucky breaks.

No One Can Give You Love

As I said earlier, when I first moved out of home, I lived in a one-bedroom apartment in Neutral Bay. The apartment was vintage 1960s, but it suited my needs at the time – especially the financial ones! The feature I remember most from my time there is the constant arguing of the couple next door. Every night they would let fly with insults – which would be interspersed with the woman begging for more love. I was astounded at how two people could put up with so much crap in their relationship and still call each other husband and wife. Some nights I even thought it was going to end violently, like one of those stories you see on TV or read in the paper.

The one thing I will never forget was the woman's constant begging for her man to love her. She was always crying for his love and demanding that he love her more. He would say, 'What more do you want from me? Blood?'

It was the same thing every night for a long time – but things changed one afternoon. There was sudden quiet. I thought to myself, 'It's only the lull before the storm. They'll be at it again before I know it.' But then the reality hit. I could hear a man's voice which didn't belong to the man who lived there. And then another guy's voice, and then another. It was a team of removalists, moving the wife out. She had finally had enough and wasn't going to put up with the situation any longer.

Only I Can Love Me

I have received many letters from readers who have shared similar nightmares to the woman in the apartment next door, some lasting as long as 15 years. One reader, Amanda, said that it was only after she spent some time in hospital for an unrelated illness that she realised how low she had fallen. While she was in hospital, an old friend from her schooldays, who was visiting from interstate, dropped by to see how Amanda was doing.

They began to chat about the time, years before, when they had shared an apartment, and laughed about all the fun times they had had there. After her friend had gone, Amanda thought about how happy she had been in those days, and how miserable her life was now. She realised that it was up to her to pick herself up and restore her self-esteem to a healthy level. She wrote, 'I have allowed this nightmare to go on for so long now that it has seemed unrealistic to expect a life of happiness. That was until I read *You Can Do It!*, when I decided that enough's enough – I was going to make a change, whether my husband liked it or not.'

The Greatest Love of All

Those famous words from Whitney Houston, 'Learning to love yourself is the greatest love of all', sum up where many people could be making a mistake. If you are attracting men or women in your life who abuse you and don't respect you, it's easy to blame them – especially when well-meaning family and friends insist that your partner is a loser whom you should never have married in the first place.

In my seminars, when people ask me to explain this concept, I refer back to the 747 aircraft. If you were flying at 35 000 feet and another 747 flew past at the same altitude, what would you see? The answer is pretty simple, isn't it? You would see the aircraft and all the passengers in it. But what if a 747 flew way above you, at 50 000 feet, or way below you, at 10 000 feet, what would you see? Again the answer is simple: you wouldn't see anything.

You are flying right now at the 'altitude' you think you deserve, and it's this 'altitude' that needs to be reset if you are to have any chance of achieving more in your life. As the 747 example clearly shows, flying at the same 'altitude' only continues to deliver into your life more of the same events and people that you have become used to.

Life is the same. Decide that you deserve better and start to lift your self-esteem, and you will suddenly find yourself flying with people and events at a new, higher altitude. It's that simple. Your attitude controls your altitude in life!

Want to know more about...?

8

Your purpose in life

Imagination is the highest kite one can fly.

LAUREN BACALL

In this chapter:

- ◆ The connection between your purpose in life and your happiness

- ◆ How to connect with your true purpose

- ◆ Having the courage to break away

- ◆ Mike's story – moving from chemist to café owner

- ◆ Why courage and conviction are two essential elements for following your dreams

W ithout doubt, you take one of the major steps in determining your level of happiness in life when you gain clarity in what is your life purpose. 'Life purpose' is hard to define as a single element, because your life is made up of work, family, health, and so on. Most people understand the term to mean the one thing they believe they are on this planet for.

You might see your purpose in life as doing community work to help the poor. Or you might believe you are here to be the best parent you can be, to bring human beings into the world and raise them as accountable members of society. Or maybe your purpose in life is totally focused towards your career and making major advances in whatever field you choose. There are no rights and wrongs here; your purpose in life is whatever you want it to be.

I knew at a very early age that I would somehow earn my living in front of an audience. On the face of that, you would guess that I might become an actor or singer. Well, if you have heard my singing, you will be glad that I became a speaker! Seriously though, I can remember the people who used to come into our grocery store, and the funny thing is that they always knew I would end up having something to do with talking.

I was visiting my mum recently and ran into one of our former neighbours. When she found out I was a speaker, she laughed and said, 'Oh my God, now they are paying you for it!' She said she had never forgotten my constant chattering in the shop, and knew that one day I would become a lawyer or solicitor or end up in some other job which involved talking a lot. I guess she was right!

How to Connect with Your True Purpose

Can you remember the last time you spent some quiet time with yourself? Listening to music and watching TV don't count – I mean some *real* quiet time. The more quiet time you spend with yourself, the more clarity you achieve and the more focused you will become towards your real purpose in life.

The feedback I have received from people attending my seminars is that they have never realised before that one of the major hurdles to gaining more clarity in their life was that they have become too busy 'even to think about it'.

I have found that when you throw yourself into your career and do your absolute best, you receive guidance from your intuition to steer you towards your purpose. All successful people I know share a similar story of how they managed to start their own business. They did their absolute best for their former employer, and by doing this gained the self-confidence needed to go out on their own.

Having the Courage to Break Away

In today's environment, it can be very hard for young people to make up their mind about their purpose in life. Many of them have parents who didn't do so well academically themselves and who have vowed their kids will 'achieve' because they did not. People from ethnic backgrounds are also likely to want their children to do better than they have. It's no accident that many of the names of the top students in end-of-year exams are Asian. Some of these kids have parents who came to Australia with nothing but the clothes on their backs and a determination to ensure that their children would never again be refugees searching for freedom in a leaky boat.

I believe that the best support a parent can give a child is the surety that whatever the child chooses to do, it will be fine by them. Many parents think that if they narrow the field by telling the kid at an early age what they expect – for example, 'Wouldn't it be nice if we had another generation of doctors in our family?' – the kid will choose that direction. This is naive. It only stuffs the kid up and delays them from realising their real purpose in life.

How many people do you know who have put years of study into chasing a goal that is not theirs, only to realise when they get to middle age that they never wanted to be a school teacher like their mum or a builder like their dad? **It takes courage and strength to chase your own goals**, and it's this that leads you to your purpose in life. You can't expect to wake up one morning and realise what your purpose in life is if for the last decade you have ignored your inner guidance.

Having come from an ethnic background, I can understand the pressure many people face. Losing my father was a devastating experience, but there was a positive side, which I have only realised in recent years. Many of the people I grew up with, who excelled at school and went on to university, are now in dead-end jobs. Most of them are complaining about how unfair life has been to them. Like me, many of these people had parents from ethnic backgrounds who wanted their children to succeed. I realised that because I did not have a father to stand over me, I could choose to do whatever I wanted. I just went with the flow and in the process found my purpose in life – and I love it to bits!

Mike and His Destiny

When I first met Mike, he was your average chemist, doing quite well. He was married with two kids, had a nice waterfront home in Brisbane and drove a Porsche Boxster to work and back. Life looked pretty good – but it wasn't. Mike's brother, Kieran, was a senior executive with a finance company which had arranged for all its people to attend my seminar. Kieran came to a seminar with his managers and then asked me if it was all right if he invited Mike along to the next seminar. I said, 'Of course,' and looked forward to meeting him.

When I first laid eyes on Mike he looked sad, but he said he was looking forward to attending the seminar as his brother had really enjoyed it. During the lunch break, Mike said he was already blown away with the content. I asked him what he had enjoyed most, and he replied that the major point for him was that he had given away his power to his parents and had surrendered all his own dreams to satisfy theirs. While he acknowledged that he had what most people would consider an enviable lifestyle, he felt like a prisoner. And he said that from that day on, things would change.

When I asked how things would change, he said that he really didn't like his job and had decided to toss it in within 60 days. He went on, 'I've always wanted to run a little café – my wife and I are both excellent cooks. In fact, she currently works part-time in a friend's sandwich shop, not because we need the money but because she loves being around people and food. We both do.'

Mike wrote to me a few weeks later to say that he and his wife were moving to a resort town north of Brisbane, where they had bought a beautiful little café. It needed some work, but had huge potential. Between the lines of his letter I could hear in Mike's voice that he had discovered his life purpose, which had only arrived after many years of pain and anxiety in a job that was far removed from what he really wanted.

Courage and Conviction

At 42 years of age, Mike is proof that it's never too late to make the change and chase what you really want in life. It takes courage and conviction at any age to chase your goals and not be swayed by the people around you. And yet again, it all comes back to self-esteem. What really determines whether or not you follow your dreams is your opinion of yourself. How you see yourself is the most fundamental point in deciding whether you listen to your inner voice or do what others expect.

Giving away a lucrative career in pharmacy for a career as a small-business owner in a café might at first seem like a risky step. But like Mike, what you will find with anyone who is guided by their inner belief is that while they admit there is a risk, they have no problem in going ahead with their commitment. They believe they will come through in the end, and that their true purpose in life is now being acted upon.

I Want to be a Fire-engine Driver

Can you remember the questions people asked you when you were in the final stages of school? Questions like: 'What are you going to do when you leave school?' and 'Are you going to do more study?'

I always found it quite remarkable, when I was young, that some kids could answer questions about what they wanted to be with clarity. Now that I am an adult, I know many of these answers were inspired by TV shows being aired at the time or encouraged by doting parents who only wanted the best for their kids. I look at my life and can say that, without a doubt, I was always meant to be a professional speaker. But when I was asked what I was going to do with my life, most people expected me to say I was going to have something to do with cars. As you have probably gathered by now, I am a big car enthusiast, but that doesn't mean I have to spend my life around them.

What decisions did you make a long time ago which are not appropriate any more? What do you need to let go of to achieve more happiness in your world? Many people write and tell me how they feel cornered in their job because of their current financial commitments. And I completely understand their dilemma. Let's say you made a decision when you were 18 to study for a law degree, because that's what your family wanted – and anyway, you didn't know what you wanted, so you decided to take the heat off your back by doing law. It sounded impressive when you told all your friends, 'I'm doing law.'

But deep inside, you love interior decorating, and just about salivate every time the new issues of *Belle* and *Vogue* arrive!

What makes you happy? What is your purpose in life? The answers to these and many more of your questions on life purpose can be found when you take some quiet time to reflect on what has made you really happy in the years leading up to where you are now. You will also find the courage to leave behind some outdated decisions that were right for you when you were 15, but are not suitable for the person you are today.

Want to know more about...?

9

Wake-up calls

Tough times never last, but tough people do.

ROBERT SCHULLER

In this chapter:

- ◆ The shock news of my mother's accident

- ◆ Touch and go for two weeks

- ◆ How dealing with this setback improved my speaking and focus

- ◆ The lessons we all learn during tough times

- ◆ Life crises and how they can be your wake-up call

Friday morning, 31 October 1997, was a beautiful spring morning. The kookaburras and cicadas were at their very loudest and I was looking forward to my normal early-morning eight-kilometre walk. I left my house at about 6 a.m. and really enjoyed the walk. On my return, I had my usual fruit salad and orange juice and prepared to get ready for a luncheon/consulting session in the city.

The Voice-mail Message – Welcome to My Nightmare

Before I left I decided to check my messages to see if any clients had called early, which is a normal occurrence and something I encourage them to do. There was one message, which had come in at 6 a.m. The time of the call struck me as a bit odd, as it was just a little too early for a client to be calling.

The message was from one of my sisters. In a sharp and emotional voice, she told me that as soon as I got the message I should contact my other sister on her mobile phone. I knew instantly that something was wrong, that someone was dead or near death. I felt my heart racing. Who was it? Were they dead? What had happened? In a desperate attempt to find out, I rang my sister, but her mobile was turned off. I then tried everyone in my family, but their mobiles were all turned off too and every home phone was ringing out. Great.

I decided to ring one of my uncles, Bill Gilbert, a down-to-earth, no-nonsense sort of guy. He broke the news to me with no carrying on, just like I wanted to hear it, straight out. He said that my mother had been involved in a head-on collision with a 19-year-old drunk driver, and was in intensive care at Liverpool Hospital.

Absolute shock descended upon me. I couldn't believe what I was hearing, and I remember thinking how quickly life can turn. One minute you're on top of the world, and the next you're feeling as low as you can go. I'd had a fantastic year with the success of my books and my business, and now my mother was lying seriously injured in hospital.

The drive from my home to the hospital is a good hour and a half normally, but I think I did it in 40 minutes after that call. I don't really remember – all I know is that it seemed to take forever. When I arrived I was told to wait in the ICU (intensive care unit) waiting lounge, where I found the rest of my family, as well as many young people I didn't know, all crying. I thought they must have been related to the poor young kid who had hit my mum, and I was right. He had just died from the injuries he received. His car had rolled ten times, then landed on top of my mum's Mazda.

While I knew Mum was battling for her own life, I could only feel sorrow for the family and friends of this young guy – we all do stupid things when we are young. Instantly, my mind flashed back to when my father had died. I knew what pain was all about and I could only feel sorry for these people, who had lost a son, brother and friend who was only 19 years of age.

We were eventually allowed into the ICU to see Mum. She looked pretty bashed up, as if she had been in a bar-room brawl. The lowdown was this: a bruised sternum, five broken ribs and a punctured breast – but my mum is a fighter, so I knew she would be okay. The next couple of days she underwent surgery for fluid on her breast, which had started an infection. The nurses kept on reassuring us that this was normal and that after a couple of days the infection would clear.

Two weeks later, Mum was still suffering high temperatures from the infection, and was going downhill fast. The following Sunday we were called to the hospital, as the medical staff thought she looked pretty bad. I was getting angry. How could this happen? Two weeks after the accident, with all the reassurances in the world, and Mum was gasping for breath.

Despite this, the rest of my family seemed happy to trust the doctors and nurses to continue their treatment. I learnt from this experience that in such situations people are generally too scared to ask the medical staff any questions and are willing to let them simply go about their job.

In any organisation, the staff are held accountable 100 per cent of the time. Yet I find in the medical field, if you start asking a doctor or nurse what course of action they are taking, you are looked on as a 'troublemaker', not a 'concerned customer'.

Touch and Go Every Night for Two More Weeks

The next day I had to do one of the hardest speaking engagements I have ever had to do, at the Parramatta Parkroyal Hotel for Aussie Home Loans. More than 1000 management and staff were coming to my sessions over the next two months and Monday was the first day of the nationwide tour.

I surprised myself at how well I went, considering what kept jumping into my head every ten minutes or so. In fact, at the end of the seminar, one of the participants told me how I had smiled a lot during it and how I must really enjoy what I do. Well, I just had to have a good belly-laugh and agree with her, but I will never forget that seminar. I said to myself that morning before going on stage that if I could get through this one, I could get through anything. I think I was right!

After every seminar, I would race back to the hospital and see how Mum was doing. For two more long weeks nothing really changed. The infections continued, as did the sleepless nights for all of us, including Mum. The 'not knowing' was the hardest. Was she going to be here in six months' time? Or was she not going to pull through?

I continued doing the Aussie Home Loans seminars around Australia, phoning Mum to see how she was doing. After about three weeks, I noticed that she was sounding stronger and more like her old self. I remember becoming very impatient with Mum's recovery because it seemed to take ages for even the most minor improvement. The saying 'Impatience implies self-doubt' kept coming back to me, and I knew that I had to keep believing that Mum was going to pull through. If I could keep holding on to that belief, my impatience would become less intense.

From reassurances that Mum would be in hospital for a week at the most, she finally returned home eight weeks later, just in time for Christmas. She is now recovering slowly, and took her first drive the other day.

The Lessons

Now, every time I see an accident on TV, my mind flashes to how close we came to losing our mum too early. I also think of the family of the young driver. The biggest lesson for me was that you have to make every moment count. You don't know when one of your parents, family or friends is going to be taken from you, so you need to seize every moment while you can.

We are often tested to believe in ourselves, and I think Mum's accident was sent not only for her, but also for me and my family.

I think it was a message to get our act together and refocus ourselves once again on what is important in our family.

More than anything else, I know that on that darkest of Sunday evenings when I was lying in bed unable to sleep, wondering whether Mum was going to die or not, the message 'believe and achieve' took on a whole different meaning.

Up to this point, I had always known the power of believe and achieve at work, because I had seen it first-hand when I was building my business. During setbacks and those days we all call 'shockers', I knew I must always believe that I was going to pull through, that I was going to make it.

But suddenly, here I was at my mother's bedside and for the first time in a long while I was starting to feel doubt and insecurity similar to what I had felt when my business was struggling. Of course, to feel the hopelessness and total lack of being able to do anything about my mother's injuries was far more devastating than any business venture. But I did think I had conquered insecurity and not believing in myself. Just when I thought I was safe, bang! From left field had come a kick in the guts like no other. While in recent times 'believing and achieving', for me, had meant getting clients and so forth, now it meant believing that Mum would pull through and achieve optimum health again.

The next time you decide to watch a video at home, consider hiring *The Doctor*, starring William Hurt. It's an excellent film about a rich, successful surgeon who gets cancer and ends up in hospital, on 'the other side of the fence'. Instead of being the one in charge, he finds himself at the mercy of unfeeling doctors and a bureaucratic hospital administration.

Sometimes we experience life crises that make us wake up to ourselves. My mother's near-fatal car accident highlighted to me again the need to make the most of every day and realise the things we take for granted in our lives. In my darkest hour on that Sunday night, when all hope seemed lost, I heard one of my favourite quotes ringing through my head: 'Tough times never last, but tough people do.'

Want to know more about...?

10

How to build passion and desire

Once a seed is planted, it never shrinks – it just grows.

HENRY DAVID THOREAU

In this chapter:

◆ Why passion and desire need nourishment to survive

◆ How to use a past success for a future goal

◆ How to go on holiday without leaving town

◆ Why music can be the best tranquilliser

◆ Having the courage to believe that the means will arrive

◆ Using feeling to move closer to your goals

Have you ever noticed that when you first decide to buy a new car or house, or begin planning a big holiday, you start getting excited?

Let's take the holiday, for example. It's 12 degrees outside and raining, and you're at home watching the footy on TV. You turn on the heater and rug up. Suddenly, the TV is awash with the turquoise-blue water of the Whitsundays. You see a couple having the time of their life doing absolutely nothing next to a massive hexagonal pool. Decked out in sunglasses and baseball caps, they are sipping on mango daiquiris and cold beer, drinking in the splendour of this tropical paradise. You have always wanted to visit this part of Australia and you start to think, 'Maybe I deserve a holiday.' The seed is planted.

It gets to half-time in the footy and now you're really feeling the cold. The telecast is sponsored by an airline which flies to this idyllic island resort, and just after you've adjusted the heater for the third time, the ad appears again, this time showing the couple enjoying the wonders of the Great Barrier Reef, swimming among the coral and loving it. You start to think seriously about taking a holiday, and decide you will call into a travel agent on the way home from work tomorrow. The seed is now not only planted, but is getting watered regularly.

On your way to work the next day, you suddenly see on the back of a bus an advertisement for that island resort. There, in full colour by the pool, is that couple from the TV ad again. You think to yourself, 'I'm definitely getting that brochure!' On visiting the travel agent, you not only get a brochure, but the agent lends you a video about the place and gives you some prices. The seed is now turning into a seedling and being fertilised very well! After you watch the video and talk to some friends who have been to the Whitsundays and had a great time, you know for sure that this is where you will take your next holiday.

Desire and Passion – Keep Watering the Seeds

Just as advertisers know that they need to repeat their ads in order to build consumers' desire for their products, you need to keep reminding yourself of your dreams and goals. **The more you remind yourself of what you want in life, the more comfortable you will become with it**. And before you know it, you're seriously considering its purchase.

Think back to the last time you planted a seed in your garden. When you plant a seed, you keep giving it as much water as it needs to grow into a beautiful flower or shrub, and wait for it to grow. You wouldn't dream of going outside the next day and expecting to see the flower as it appeared on the seed packet, would you? You wouldn't go back to the plant nursery and demand your money back because the flower didn't grow overnight!

Sadly, this is the approach many people take with their dreams and goals. They try various methods to achieve them overnight, such as gambling on the lottery, the pokies, the horses or the dogs. They spend their time forever chasing the instant riches which have always eluded them. It's all too easy to start something and wonder why after a while your enthusiasm is not pumping as much as it should be, why your desire has conked out and you're running on empty. To build desire and passion for anything, you have to regularly 'water' your 'seeds' – and after a short time, you will see a beautiful plant.

One way of doing this is via mental rehearsal, or visualisation. It's a powerful technique that can greatly assist you to remain centred and focused during your journey.

As you know by now, how you see yourself is the one determining factor that will decide whether you achieve your full potential. You have two choices when it comes to changing how you feel about yourself. You can sit around hoping for a fairy godmother to touch you on the shoulder and make everything all right, or you can take personal control of your life and use techniques such as mental rehearsal to reaffirm your belief that you can achieve.

Mental Rehearsal – Seven Easy Tips

Tip 1 – A Past Success

Remember the time you won an event at the school sporting carnival? How did you feel when you were awarded that blue ribbon for coming first? Or what about when you walked up the aisle to get married? Did you feel on top of the world? You can use key events such as this to bring more happiness and success into your life. Sporting stars know the power of flicking back to a past grand final win and how they felt doing the lap of honour. They revisit how they felt when the crowd was cheering and waving banners and relive the emotion of carrying the trophy around the stadium.

Can you think of past events, right now, which make you feel good? This is a very effective tool and one that will ensure that your past successes are always with you.

Tip 2 – Go for a Holiday ... in Your Mind!

Top achievers know that one of the keys to winning in life is to stay on top of things. With everything happening so fast around you, it's good to know you can go on a holiday any time you want. Yes, you read right – any time you want!

Allow yourself some quiet time to revisit a favourite holiday destination. Remember your favourite view or scene and picture it in your mind. In my case, when I find myself getting frustrated or tense I travel to Glacier Bay National Park in Alaska, where I had a fabulous holiday a few years ago. When my mind flicks back to the magnificent spectacle of snow and ice turning orange in the setting sun, I start to feel my tension slipping away.

Tip 3 – Music Calms the Soul

This is one of the quickest ways to relax and achieve a state of calm. When you listen to music, your brain starts to operate on a different wavelength. Loud music will put you into a high state of readiness, while quiet background music will slow down your thinking and allow you to focus on the sounds you are hearing.

Try listening to 'environmental' music, such as the sounds of a rainforest or ocean. As you focus on the calls of the birds or the crashing of the waves, your mind will quieten and the stress will start to float away. Achievers know that when they let go of the stress in their mind, they make 'landing space' for the new opportunities circling above them.

Tip 4 – Know that the Means Will Arrive

One of the most important steps in achieving a more relaxed state – and thus a more productive frame of mind – is to understand that the means for your goals will arrive in time to achieve your dreams. This is where non-attachment comes in (see Chapter 12). It's setting your goals and then letting go of the panicky 'How-am-I-going-to-achieve-this?' feeling. When you truly believe this concept, it does work. It's no good saying 'I'll give it a go' and then approaching it with scepticism. You really have to believe that 'the way will be shown' to you. You need to **have faith in you**.

Tip 5 – Repetition Reinforces Calm

At the centre of most meditation techniques is the mantra. What is a mantra? Very simply, it is repeating a sound to yourself again and again. Some Eastern religions suggest sounds like 'um' or 'mmm'. When you repeat the sound over and over, you find you are no longer focusing on your worries – just on that sound.

You can also use this ancient form of meditation to reinforce an emotion or state you want to achieve in life. Some people repeat 'calm calm calm calm' as they go off to sleep. I know one business-man who for the last 20 years has drifted off to sleep saying, 'Wealth wealth wealth wealth'. It's up to you which word you use, but be assured that its impact will be felt as long as you keep up the reinforcement.

Tip 6 – Feeling is Believing

Here is a wonderful technique that uses all your senses. If there is something you want to buy, such as a house or car, try seeing, touching, even smelling it and you will find it easier to achieve your desire.

Arthur was never a good saver of money – until he discovered this technique. He wanted to buy a new car, and in order to prepare himself, he visited as many car dealerships as he could on weekends. He would sit behind the wheel and smell the aroma that only a new car can provide, and let his senses slowly adjust to what became a regular experience. When he decided on the make he wanted, he started visiting that franchise's dealers not only to get prices, but to let his senses get excited again. Arthur told me he was now closer than ever before to owning his new car and was amazed at how the constant visits to dealers had kept him focused.

What are you currently finding hard to achieve? Use this technique and watch your senses take over.

Tip 7 – Feel the Feeling

'Feel the feeling' might sound strange when you see it in words, but it's actually a great way to reinforce a desirable trait or attract something in your life. The idea is to imagine that you already have the thing you desire. How would you feel? What emotions would you experience?

Sit in a quiet place at home for 20 minutes and pretend you already have the object, state or emotion you have been wanting. Remember, the subconscious cannot tell the difference between a real event and a vividly imagined event, so the more you focus on those positive feelings, the more successful you will be in attracting what you want.

It's been said that the main function of the body is to carry the head around! The more I learn about the power of the mind, the more I know that we all have much more to give. Many people are looking 'outside' for solutions to their challenges, when for the most part the answers lie within them.

Don't make the mistake of running after 'instant solutions'. Don't rip yourself off by wasting your money on quick fixes – there aren't any. Instead, plant a seed of desire for what you want in the future and nurture it with as much self-esteem as you can muster. Then you will achieve it. Take some quiet time in the next week to try at least one of the tips in this chapter. I know you won't be disappointed.

Want to know more about...?

11

You can lose it! (Weight, that is.)

We are what we repeatedly do.

ARISTOTLE

In this chapter:

- ◆ You have to want to get healthy

- ◆ Changing your diet to achieve your weight-loss goal

- ◆ Exercise – the missing link in most people's lives

- ◆ How to make time when you're too busy

- ◆ How to break through the terrible feeling of plateauing out

- ◆ Fruit, vegetables and good health – it's that easy

- ◆ Why drinking water assists losing weight

- ◆ Why coffee and tea have to go

- ◆ You can think yourself thinner . . . if you want to

'And please give a big *Midday* welcome to Australia's king of motivation, Paul Hanna!' With those words, my life was about to change forever. *You Can Do It!* was launched in May 1997 on *The Midday Show with Kerri-Anne Kennerley*, Australia's number-one daytime TV show. An amazing thing happened to me on that show. **I saw myself**.

Yes, that's right, I saw myself.

With TV engagements and radio interviews booked one after another, my publishers wanted to make sure they seized every moment to market the book. Forget the publishers – *I* wanted to seize every moment as well! This was 'make or break' for me and I had to make it work. After an amazing two weeks of interviews for the electronic and paper media, I was relaxing at a friend's place over dinner when someone at the table said they had seen me on *The Midday Show*. I hadn't seen the telecast, and neither had some of the other guests, but my friend had taped it – so after dinner we watched it. When I saw myself, I was so chubby I couldn't believe my eyes. After more than 12 months writing my book, I had let myself slip. It has been said that television adds another 6 kilos of weight to people – but forget that. I was overweight and didn't like what I saw.

I knew that, in addition to gaining weight, I had lost a lot of energy. Something had to give. With the success of my book, and a speaking schedule that was getting busier every year, I was at a crossroads in my life. There and then I decided I would start to look after myself better on a physical *and* mental level.

The Commitment – 18 Kilos by Christmas

After the book tour was over, I started to focus on my lifestyle. What was I eating? How much exercise was I doing? How much water did I drink? I set myself a goal of losing 18 kilos by Christmas. It was a big challenge. If I was to lose that much weight, I would have to take advantage of every week of the seven months remaining.

The first thing I did was read every book I could find on diet and lifestyle. I wanted to see how much junk there was in my life and what I would have to give up. The second thing was to make a commitment from day one to exercise every day, no matter what.

I want to share with you some of the highlights of what I learnt as I watched the kilos fall off me every day. How I challenged the plateaus and brought my body to a healthier level than I had ever known.

Changing My Diet

With 90 per cent of my consulting being conducted in restaurants just before, just after or during a meal, I thought I would have my work cut out trying to lose weight. I mean, how could I possibly lose weight eating out so often?

Among all the books I read, the one that stands out as the easiest and most down-to-earth is a little gem called *Fit for Life* by Harvey and Marilyn Diamond. I had purchased this terrific book about two years earlier and remembered reading it on a flight somewhere, but for whatever reason did not take up the challenge. It wasn't until after the launch of *You Can Do It!* that I heard those magic words: 'Enough's enough!'

I always hope that readers will get at least one thing out of my books – just one point for home or work and the book will have been worth it. I learnt many things from the diet and lifestyle books I read, and they were so easy to put into my hectic lifestyle that the kilos just fell away. Some of the highlights follow. I should say here that while these worked for me, everyone is different. If you don't see results with this method, keep reading until you find a book that suits you. And always remember to consult your doctor before you begin any diet or exercise program, just to make sure it's okay for you to do it.

1. Eat only fruit before midday.

This is the biggest point, and the one that is the easiest to commit to. The changes I felt in my body almost immediately were incredible. And the scariest thing about my whole eating pattern up to this point was that, looking back over the last two to three years, I couldn't remember eating *any* fruit in my diet. None!

There are no excuses for this. Every hotel I have stayed in since commencing my new lifestyle has accommodated my requests. Qantas and Ansett have the best fruit and vegetable meals you can get – they are fresh as fresh. But you have to do one thing – you have to ask for them!

2. Proper food combining.

This one is a real beauty. Food combining is based on the principle that eating the right combinations of foods leads to better digestion and improved health and energy levels. When I first read about it, I thought, 'How could something so important not be taught to us at school?' Here are a few pointers that really helped me.

- When you eat foods that don't combine well, you force your body to go into overdrive to sort them out, which takes up energy you could use for other things. Before you know it, you're getting tired and irritable. It's important to know this, because **the cornerstone to any weight-loss program is energy**. Some foods that should never be eaten together are eggs and toast; cheese and bread; breakfast cereal and milk; and chicken and noodles.
- Reduce all meat and dairy products in your diet. This is an important point, because while I had been a vegetarian for at least five years, as well as eating very few dairy products, I was still carrying a lot of excess weight. To me, this highlights the point that it is not how much you eat, but what you eat that really counts.
- Fruit must be eaten on an empty stomach.
- Wait for at least two hours after eating fruit, before you consume anything else. The reverse applies as well: don't eat fruit until at least two hours have passed since your last meal.
- Invest in a juicer. I did have one, but it sat in the bottom of my pantry at home until I discovered that I could make some excellent fruit juices to satisfy my cravings during the long and sometimes hungry hours writing this book!

How I Made Exercise Work for Me

After having more than 6 kilos of weight fall off just by watching what I was eating, I thought to myself, 'How can I not only keep it off, but lose more?'

Around this time I was speaking in Coolum on Queensland's Sunshine Coast. I decided to take a few days of well-earned R & R in nearby Noosa Heads. I visited the local bookstore and, after chatting to the owner for a while, decided to buy a book that would assist in taking me to the next level of weight loss and health. I discovered the *Gutbuster Waist Loss Guide* by Australians Rosemary Stanton and Garry Egger. Most of us have heard about the success of the Gutbuster program, but I had never really found out what it is they do to lose the gut!

In this book I found many good ideas, but one thing that really hit me was the point made about the link between walking and health. If you are like me, you have probably heard for years now about the need to do some form of exercise at least three times a week for at least 20 minutes. Two weeks before I went to Coolum, I had started to walk for 15 minutes every morning. This might not sound like much of a commitment, but I had been amazed how, with such little effort, I started feeling better.

The *Gutbuster Waist Loss Guide* made the point that **you can do exercise for** *fitness* **or** *fatness*. This struck a chord because it explained why I'd been having trouble losing weight over the last two years despite undertaking a fitness program. To fill you in, about two years before, I had realised my weight was starting to build up. Little things like hiring formal wear for special occasions would always be a gentle reminder; the suit I fitted into last time would now not fit. So I decided to hire a personal trainer. I know this sounds very 'Hollywood', but I was desperate to regain my energy levels of five years before – and the waist that went with it. After more than six months with the trainer, using weights and walking on a treadmill every second day, I had lost very little weight.

Then my trainer was snapped up by a wealthy Kuala Lumpur industrialist, who asked him to come and live with them and set up their own personal gym. When the trainer left, he gave me the names of some of his mates, whom he said were just as good, but seeing very little result from my six months' hard work, I decided to leave it and see if I could do it by myself. Well, two years passed and the weight built up – which brought me to the point of 'Enough's enough'.

When I read about fitness and fatness, it became obvious. Here I was trying to lose *fat*, but what I was actually doing was exercising to get *fit*. Now while I am the first to agree that getting fit is important, what I really wanted to do was lose weight. And after all, it's a lot easier to get fit when you are 6 kilos lighter, wouldn't you agree?

Eight Kilometres Every Morning – No Excuses

When I returned from Noosa, I decided I would start to increase my walking a little at a time. I gradually went from 15 minutes to 20 minutes to 30 minutes, then 45, then 60. Now, I walk every morning for one hour 16 minutes exactly, which allows me to cover eight kilometres.

I can't put into words how euphoric I feel every time I return from my walk. Not only am I losing weight, but the walking has done incredible things for my speaking as well. I always knew my energy had been slipping over the years, but to have all that energy back plus 50 per cent more is truly incredible. No personal trainers; no sweating it out with the 'glamour set' at the local gym. Here I am, on my own terms, walking among the trees and birds I have taken for granted for so long.

The crazy thing is this: I reckon I could now eat anything and my weight would stay where it is. Because I walk every morning without fail – rain, hail or shine – I have found that my appetite has increased and my energy has gone through the roof. I thought my seminars were going pretty well *before* I lost all that excess weight, but I have been absolutely astounded at how much more I can give now. By 'giving', I mean I can give more of me (or is it less of me?!). I am able to connect with my audiences on an even higher plane – one which I have never reached before.

I Don't Have Enough Time – I'm Too Busy

How many times have you used the line 'I'm too busy' or 'You don't understand my lifestyle; I just don't have a spare minute to exercise'? I have used both of these and others, but the bottom line is this: do you want to lose weight or not? If the answer is 'Yes, yes, yes!', the following few tips might help you. They have certainly assisted me on the path to achieving better health.

Tip 1 – Get up early.

Ask anyone who has written a book, and they will probably tell you that the most productive time to write is in the early hours of the morning. This is when the mind is most relaxed; you've just had a good night's sleep and you're focused and ready to go. For my first two books, I knew I had to find extra time in my hectic lifestyle if I was going to meet my contractual obligations to Penguin, so I decided to try getting up earlier. While at first it took a bit of acclimatising, it worked out very well. I would find myself going to bed at about 9.30 p.m. and getting up between 4 and 5 a.m. depending on my schedule.

Just as your body acclimatises when you fly overseas to a new time zone, so it will if you start to get up one hour earlier every day. If you make it a habit, your body will have to compensate in some way to give you enough energy to get through the day. To get back the energy you have lost by getting up earlier in the morning, your body will start to make you tired one hour earlier in the evening. After about a week, you will see your sleeping rhythms adjusting to your new schedule. When I saw how easy it was to find the extra hours I needed to write, I thought, 'Why not do the same for my health?' If I could get up earlier than I normally did to write a book, why couldn't I maintain that habit and walk for an hour and a half? After all, what was at stake was something much more important than a book – my health.

Tip 2 – Break through the plateaus.

Let me give you a scenario. You decide to start eating fruit only before midday. Recognising it has an easy opportunity to get rid of some excess flab, your body goes into overdrive to lose the excess weight while it can. It thinks you're going to return to the steak-and-eggs diet it has been conditioned to receive for most of its life, so it's not going to take this opportunity for granted. Depending on how overweight you are, you will see a quick loss of weight start to happen within two weeks.

But after about two weeks, your body realises you are serious. You are not going back to eggs Benedict every morning (my former favourite!) and you are committed to a healthy lifestyle. Sensing this, your body decides to take it easy, because it has lost that sense of urgency now that it has realised it has a whole lifetime to take off the weight. After all, the excess did not come on over-night – it was the same process, reversed. I noticed this happening when I lost my first stage of weight. I plateaued out and stopped losing it.

The time has come to make your exercise 'inefficient'. But why on earth would you want to do this? Like you, I thought that to lose weight, I should be seeking out *efficient* exercises. But as I read more, I discovered that the body is always wanting to be challenged. It wants constantly to strive for improvement or it will plateau out. This is when 'inefficient' exercise really kicks in, because the body is now seeking a new challenge.

To get the body back to that sense of urgency, you need con-stantly to add to and alter your exercise program. When I started walking, I gradually increased the distance. But after getting to eight kilometres every morning, I looked at new, fun ways to make a difference. Sometimes I change the route; sometimes I change the fruit I eat in the morning; and sometimes I mix and change the fruit juices I drink.

Tip 3 – Walk somewhere different.

Port Douglas, in Far North Queensland, is a popular convention destination and I am fortunate to be asked to speak there many times a year. On a recent visit, I decided to walk along Four Mile Beach, which is where the Sheraton Mirage is located. Now while I have had the opportunity to visit this magnificent resort before, any spare time I had in the past was always spent around the resort's massive salt-water lagoons. On this trip, I decided I would do my walk up and down Four Mile Beach.

Every morning, I woke up at 4 a.m. and walked along what would have to be one of the most spectacular beaches in the world. At 5.30, when the sun rises above the calm waters of the beach, you think you could walk all day. It might sound pretty easy, but let me tell you it's a great shock to the body to walk barefoot on sand after you're used to walking in jogging shoes on hard road surfaces. But I really enjoyed the change!

As soon as I returned to Sydney, I made a commitment to visit the beach at least once a week and walk my eight kilometres on the sand, to kick-start my body and watch the sunrise at this beautiful time of the morning. If you don't live near a beach, find a park – all of Australia's capital cities are blessed with superb urban parks which make us the envy of the world, such as Centennial Park in Sydney, the Botanic Gardens in Melbourne and Brisbane and Kings Park in Perth.

Tip 4 – Consider 'fundays' of fruit or juice only.

This is a tip from *Fit for Life*. If you want to feel really light – and who doesn't? – have a go at an all-fruit or all-juice 'funday'. With a little preparation the day before, you will find that your body absolutely craves the fruit or juice, or both, and quickly starts to detoxify itself of all the pollutants in your body.

I find these fundays essential at least once a month, and always give them a go when my schedule is a bit slower. Don't try a funday for the first time in the middle of a hectic work week. Give it a try on a Sunday, when you are relaxing and reading the papers.

Tip 5 – Drink heaps of water.

As a speaker, I tend to drink a lot of water because I am on stage nearly every day and I need to keep in good voice. Whether it's a 45-minute keynote presentation, a half-day seminar or a full-day seminar, I find myself guzzling glass after glass of water to assist my throat and feeling of wellbeing. But until I read up on the subject, I didn't realise the power of water in my life off-stage.

Water helps your body to wash away all the impurities that have built up by assisting the liver and bowel to rid them from your body. A shortage of this simple yet powerful liquid in your body can cause problems such as constipation and lethargy. You might be sceptical that something as easy as drinking more water could improve your health so much, but think about this: over 70 per cent of the planet is water, and up to 80 per cent of the human body is made up of water. I think there's a message in that!

I now **drink at least eight to ten glasses of water a day** – which is not really a lot when you consider the smallest bottle of mineral water available at all delicatessens and corner stores these days. When you break it up, all you have to do is have at least two glasses in the morning, three around lunch time and three sometime between lunch and when you retire for the night. Easy!

Tip 6 – Kick the coffee habit.

Ask anyone who knows me, and they'll tell you I used to *love* long black coffees. Like any habit, I just drank it without thinking. But after finding out that caffeine is not very good for you, I gave it up. Caffeine stimulates both your nervous system and your appetite, so if you want a calmer, healthier lifestyle, coffee is one of the first things you might consider axing. Don't suddenly go off your cappuccino or long black tomorrow, though; do it gradually and you'll find kicking the habit that much easier.

I found that I didn't miss the coffee so much as the need to have something to drink. I needed to find a substitute drink, and I chose peppermint tea, because I remembered reading that it is a natural diuretic. This means that it assists the body to pass water more quickly and thereby gets rid of pollutants in your body faster. On the other hand, coffee – and more importantly, caffeine – is a stimulant and increases your appetite. These days, when I am asked what I would like to follow a meal, I always request peppermint tea.

Tip 7 – Be aware of your family conditioning.

What are some of the beliefs you were given at home about eating? Were you always told to finish everything on your plate? If so, can you imagine the tremendous pressure on you, every time you eat at a restaurant, to finish what is in front of you?

In my family, exercise wasn't really a big thing, hence most of my brothers and sisters have had a battle with the bulge for as long as I can remember. One of the funniest things I can remember is a friend saying, 'You must all be big-boned.' I thought it was a cop-out then, and now I know it is! We didn't have big bones, only beliefs that conditioned us to eat when we were under stress – which is exactly what happened. Living above a grocery store in the western suburbs of Sydney as we did, you can imagine what it was like coming home from school and walking through a shop full of food and drink, all for free. If we wanted something after hours it wasn't a problem either, because all we had to do was grab the key, go downstairs and raid the Paddle Pops or Twisties. Hardly a healthy lifestyle! It was one that I believe could have killed me before I was 40. My dad had died at 52, so when I got serious about my eating habits, I knew it was 'Change, or else.'

Tip 8 – Read as much as you can.

The more I read about changing my lifestyle, the more I realised how much I didn't know. Take accountability for your health and invest in at least three books that will assist you in making the right decisions. You could start with *Fit for Life* and the *Gutbuster Waist Loss Guide*, which I referred to earlier. I am not on a commission here! It's just that both these books talk plain English and contain easy-to-use ideas.

Tip 9 – Know that 'vegetarian' does not necessarily mean 'healthy'.

Some people think that if they change to a vegetarian diet they will automatically lose weight. This is not the case. I have been a vegetarian for about five years, and rarely eat dairy products. I eat chicken now and then and the occasional shaved parmesan on pasta or a caesar salad, but basically I eat a vegetarian diet. The important thing to remember is that although I was a vegetarian three years ago, I still retained all that excess weight. So don't think that by going vegetarian you will suddenly lose weight. I think it's the opposite – start to eat properly and you will find that you enjoy vegetarian food as a life-force and energy booster.

Tip 10 – Think yourself thin.

Wishful thinking, you say? Well, you're right. I truly believe that you can think yourself thin. Over the course of a day, try counting how many times you tell yourself how great you look, and how many times you tell yourself what's wrong with you. As you learnt in *You Can Do It!*, we all move towards and become like whatever we are thinking about the most. What are you thinking more about – good health or what is currently aching? A trim body or an overweight one? You are moving in the direction of your thoughts. If you want to change your physical look, first change your mental outlook. The rest will literally fall into place.

Want to know more about...?

12

Non-attachment – letting go to grow

Life is like an airport runway. You have to make space constantly so new opportunities can land.

PAUL HANNA

In this chapter:

- ◆ Non-attachment – letting go to attract better things in your life

- ◆ Time to clean out your physical world

- ◆ Brett's story – why he moves every two years

- ◆ Relationships and non-attachment

- ◆ Why doing things on your own is okay

- ◆ Robin and Justine's story – stop moulding others to be like you

- ◆ Why letting go of past mistakes can be a freeing experience

- ◆ Russell's story – how a lost promotion created 'more'

- ◆ Carla and Barry's story – letting go of excess baggage

- ◆ Matt's story – from lousy school grades to high achiever

T he universe is amazing when you really think about it. Look around you – everywhere there are marvels happening. Birds are singing and flying from tree to tree *without really trying*. The ocean waves don't *try* to crash on the sand; they just crash. And the great white shark doesn't try to swim; it just moves gracefully through the depths of the ocean. Earth and the other planets in the solar system are moving at enormous speeds, yet they don't collide with each other. **The universe has provided for everything to exist in pure harmony, including you**.

This chapter is about something called 'non-attachment'. It's about not basing your worth on the things and people around you, but letting go of things and giving people the space to journey through life as they see fit. Just as the blood in your body requires no obstructions in order to flow freely, so does your life in general. When you allow non-attachment to enter your life, you start to let new opportunities move into your life.

To fully embrace non-attachment, you have to really believe in yourself. You have to know in your heart that the universe is going to deliver. This can be a very scary thing to do, because you have to believe – without any evidence – that you are going to make it happen. When you bring it back to basics, non-attachment is about trusting yourself and the universe to provide for you. It's believing in yourself and knowing that you will become successful at whatever you choose to do. More than anything else, non-attachment is letting go of the need to control everything.

Letting Go to Attract More

We hold on to objects because we think we might lose them in the future. The same goes for people – we hold on to them because we think we might lose them. But when you try to hold on to things and people, you're setting yourself up for pain. What you're really saying is that you don't trust the universe to provide you with what you need, so you are taking every step you can to make sure you hang on to what you do have.

Society has conditioned us to become obsessed with 'owning' things: houses, cars, boats and partners – and this is how many people get their feeling of self-worth. The absolute irony is that because they have lost faith in the universe to provide for them, they end up hoarding whatever it is they have. In a sense, they stop any future growth because they have stopped the free flow of energy into their lives. Take relationships, for instance. When you hold on to a relationship, it stops growing from that point. Both partners become too reliant on each other, and give away their personal power. True non-attachment in any healthy relationship requires each partner to provide a commitment on a daily basis, so they can both grow together.

I have seen the power of non-attachment most noticeably in my business. Let's say I am working with a large corporation and 1000 people attend my seminars over a two-month period. When I am working with them, I give 100 per cent and more. I really want to make a difference and am totally focused. After the seminars are complete, I have two choices. I can do more work with the same corporation – which is always a fantastic and rewarding thing to do – or I can move on to work with another organisation. The remarkable thing is that if I decide to move on, another corporation appears, as if on cue, saying they want me to work with them.

I think back to my early days and remember the struggle I had juggling my seminars as well as trying to obtain more business. I know now that I was trying too hard. I was blocking the free flow of energy and always had a lean period following a series of seminars. But now the calendar just seems to fill, as if 'naturally'.

Clean Out Your Cupboards

One of the best ways to understand the power of non-attachment is to start with a small project. Next weekend, say, make a commitment to clean out your wardrobe and bundle up all the clothes you haven't worn for more than 12 months. Go through all those old sweaters you no longer wear which are taking up space; get rid of the ties you bought two years ago which you never wear now.

Then think of that old furniture cluttering your storage area or garage. What are you saving it for? Clear out what you don't need, then give St Vincent de Paul or the Smith Family a call and make an appointment for them to come and collect the stuff.

Most of us keep things like this, not even thinking about why we do it. A drive through any Australian suburb on a weekend will surely provide proof that people doubt their own capabilities and do not believe the universe will provide for them. Ask someone why they are having a garage sale and they'll say they wanted to get rid of all the junk lying around their house – and make some money! They pay for ads in the classifieds to attract buyers, spend a whole weekend protecting all the goods in case of theft, and make a bit of money.

But what if they knew about the law of non-attachment? What could have happened in their world if they had just given it all away? What would the universe have delivered after they had removed all that clutter in their life? You can be assured of one thing: as soon as you finish your clean-up and donate your clothes and unwanted furniture to a local charity, you will have set up the universe to deliver more into your world.

Brett Moves Every Two Years

Brett, an accountant, had attended one of my seminars in Sydney. He loved the discussion on non-attachment because it was a concept he had believed in but hadn't really understood before. He told me: 'Over the last ten years, I have moved house every two years. I love it; I feel it keeps me on my toes mentally and financially. Every time I move I have a massive clean-out and give a lot of my unwanted clothes and things to charity. I didn't realise before what I was doing, but now I can see that I'm opening the door for more in my life. I look at some of my friends who have been in the same apartment or house for ten years, and I can see why they're feeling stale and edgy. The best part of moving every two years is the fun of looking forward to the next environment I'll be living in and the new people I'll meet.'

For Brett, true non-attachment is trusting life and knowing it will deliver the very best for him.

Non-attachment and Relationships

Do you know a couple who are never apart? They're almost literally glued to each other, and don't seem to be able to go anywhere or do anything without their partner by their side.

Now don't get me wrong – I think it's terrific when you see a couple in love walking along together, but that's not what I'm talking about. I'm talking about the power of non-attachment in relationships. Many relationships flounder because one or both partners have stopped growing. They have literally moulded their two personalities into one and now can't separately stand on their own feet.

It's Okay to Do Things on Your Own

Owen and Gabriela, who attended one of my seminars last year, realised the power of non-attachment and its absence in their relationship. Gabriela said that the longer they had been married, the more insular they had become. For example, if they were invited to a social event, they would either attend it together or not at all. She went on, 'I began to notice that our tastes were usually the same, but not always. If we got invited to something and one of us didn't want to go, we ended up having a major discussion about whether we should go or not. We never thought about going to things alone. Instead, the one who didn't want to go would get dragged along like a sulky child, and after a couple of hours, just as the party was warming up, would start to whinge about going home.'

Gabriela said that she and Owen both realised that if their marriage was to survive and get back some of the excitement of the early years, they would have to let go of each other a bit. Their reward would be a partner who was more free, and – with a bit of luck! – more loving.

Robin and Justine's Story

Justine works for a major Australian corporation and attended my seminar with her husband, Robin, a dentist. When we came to the area of non-attachment, Justine started getting teary. No one else noticed, but I could see as I glanced around the room that something had upset her. I continued discussing non-attachment with the group, and then we broke for afternoon tea.

I went up to Justine and Robin to see if she was all right, but by this time, she was beaming. She said that the subject of non-attachment had hit the mark regarding their relationship. They had been married for more than five years, and things had started to get pretty tense. Justine said she could now see that she was trying to mould Robin to be more like her – which is not why she married him! Robin interrupted and said, 'It's not a one-way street. I'm guilty of the same thing.'

He said that when they were first married, he was always off with his mates during the weekend playing golf while Justine would be doing her thing with her friends. But after being with each other for five years they had lost the spontaneity in the relationship, the wanting to be together – because they had smothered the very traits they were attracted to when they first met.

Justine and Robin made a commitment that day to give each other space and to let their true selves shine through.

Letting Go of Past Mistakes

We all make mistakes – it's as much a part of life as breathing, walking and talking. Yet many people dwell on their past mistakes, making them out to be terrible events which must never be forgotten. But mistakes are just another name for 'growth experiences'; they are necessary in order for us to grow. If you don't make mistakes in your life, you will never grow beyond where you are now.

For example, you could stay in the same job for ten years and be 'perfect' at it – but the payoff is that by staying in that job you will miss the opportunities that are waiting for you. Maybe you need to change your views on 'mistakes' and look at them as ways to stretch yourself.

He 'Failed' as a General Manager but Grew as a Person

Russell is one of the top luxury-car salespeople in Australia. About eight years ago, the general manager of the dealership where Russell worked suddenly resigned because of ill health. Russell was going so well as a sales manager that the owner of the dealership immediately offered him the position of general manager. Now, while Russell knew he was doing a good job as a sales manager, he was secretly unsure how he would handle the 'big one'. But the new salary and car were just too tempting, so he accepted on the spot.

After the 'honeymoon period' was over, Russell began to struggle with the job and quickly lost confidence in himself. The whole dealership staff found the stress and tension too much, and after about eight months Russell was asked to step aside for a new general manager whom the owner had recruited from another car dealership. Russell was devastated. How could his life go from being 'cushy' to a total disaster – which was now also affecting his relationship?

After a couple of weeks off to get himself back together, Russell agreed to return to his old job of sales manager, a job he performed outstandingly well. Everyone was thrilled to see him back 'where he belonged'. But the trauma of messing up that rare opportunity to become a general manager clouded Russell's thinking for years to come. He had grown tremendously during the period he was in the job, and while he admitted that he had been out of his depth, he also knew he had learnt a lot.

Recently, the general manager who took over from Russell decided to move on. He nominated Russell as his successor, but Russell said he didn't want anything to do with it. Even though it was eight years ago, the scars were still too raw, both at home and at work, and he wasn't going to put his wife and himself through another humiliating experience like that.

The owner could understand Russell's dilemma, but insisted he talk it over with his wife and think about it for a day or two. After more than a week of lengthy discussions with his wife, the departing general manager and the owner, Russell realised he was now a different person to eight years ago. Since his last attempt at the general manager's role, he had married, had two kids and not only developed his sales team but also further developed his skills as a leader.

Russell finally accepted the position of general manager and is now one of the most successful GMs the company has had. When

I asked him what the turning point was, he replied, 'Without doubt, it was when I lost the role the first time round. It not only made me hungrier for success, but also taught me to see others going further than they currently see themselves, and then help them get there.'

For Russell, one of the biggest 'mistakes' of his life turned out to be the springboard to his future success. What past 'growth experiences' are you clouding as 'mistakes'? Maybe you need to do what Russell did – let go of the 'mistake' and grab the opportunity you are being prepared for!

The One that Got Away

Carla, a mother of five, approached me at the end of a seminar. She said she had never heard anything like it before and was surprised at how so much of the material had hit the mark for her, especially the message about letting go of past mistakes.

Carla went on to tell me about the 'baggage' she had been carrying around for more than ten years. Just after they had their third child, her husband, Barry, had suggested they invest in a larger house. Concerned by the debt they already had with their bank, Carla became nervous and told Barry she didn't really like the idea. Barry kept on insisting that the house they had inspected two weeks earlier would be ideal, as they could renovate it in the short term and auction it off later to investors. But for Carla, the scenario was all too familiar. Her father had had a similar idea when she was a kid, but had lost everything. She said she could still remember everyone crying as they packed their belongings to move out of their home into a smaller, rented house.

Eventually Barry got fed up with pestering Carla and decided to quit looking. He knew it was going to be a near-impossible task to get her into more debt. Barry went to the auction of the house and was bitterly disappointed as the house eventually sold for $50 000 less than they had thought they might have to pay. What made matters worse was that the young couple who bought the house sold it three years later for a six-figure profit, one that Barry knew was his and Carla's. Carla said that this incident caused a great deal of anxiety in their relationship, and she has always reminded herself of it every time a decision has had to be made.

After attending my seminar, Carla said she had realised that 'comfort zones' had played a big part in her decision and if she had known this then, things would have been totally different. Her childhood experience of watching her father lose everything had never really left her, and the pain of that single event had left a scar on her and on her family. Until the crisis of the decision about purchasing this house, she had not realised how much she was being held back by her comfort zone, or lower cruising altitude, in regard to money.

Carla phoned me about two months after the seminar to update me on what had happened after she discussed the matter with Barry. She said, 'We both realised we were blowing the past event out of all proportion – there are many properties available now that we could renovate and sell at a profit. We've been too busy looking behind, instead of focusing on where we want to go.'

I Did Lousy at School – Big Deal!

I met Matt at a sales convention on the Gold Coast. He was the third-highest sales achiever in his company and was loving his job. As soon as I met him I knew he was a star performer – he had that look about him that says, 'I am enjoying life and want heaps more of it.'

He said he had really enjoyed my material and found the part on letting go of past mistakes especially applicable. He had bombed out big-time in his Year 12 exams and knew all along that his destiny was not in the academic world. He was heartened by the fact that one of his uncles had left school with no formal qualifications and was now a multimillionaire. Both Matt's parents were academically inclined, and they had applied so much pressure on him to study during his final years at school that he felt he could handle anything. Matt said he was amazed at how much emphasis the media put on Year 12 results: 'Once you're in a job, your employer doesn't give a damn about what score you got – they just want high performance.'

At a recent five-year school reunion, Matt was staggered by how many of the guys he had been at school with were in 'average' jobs. The star pupils who had achieved top grades were mostly still waiting for the 'big break' in their career. In the meantime he had created his own career in sales. He had done so well that he had recently put a deposit on a beachside apartment.

Matt told me, 'Some of the mates I still go out with, who performed badly in the HSC, look back all the time at this event as the reason why they're not going well in life. But some of them are starting to realise that what counts is their attitude to what they are going to do from now on. The irony of it all is that I can't even remember my score now – and my mates don't remember theirs either!'

How much room have you made in your life for new opportunities? How much are you clinging to the past when you could be looking forward towards all the things that lie ahead of you? Whereabouts in your life is there so much clutter that there is no space for new opportunities to land?

Start clearing the decks now, in all areas of your life, to allow more possibilities to enter your thinking. At the same time, watch the sheer power of non-attachment deliver more joy and happiness than you ever thought possible.

Want to know more about...?

13

To give is to receive

What goes around comes around.

ANONYMOUS

In this chapter:

- ◆ How a petrol station incident left me on a high

- ◆ Claudia's story – how paying the toll has been a wise investment

- ◆ Swapping a business-class seat for an economy seat

- ◆ How lunches helped build my business

- ◆ Restaurants and tips – they love them

- ◆ Troy's story – how he restored 'giving and receiving' to his marriage

One Christmas Eve, I stopped at a petrol station to fill up my car. When I approached the counter to pay for the fuel, a woman in her thirties burst into the shop, gasping and looking as white as a ghost. She told the cashier that she had left home in a hurry because one of her children was sick and she needed to take him to a medical centre. The problem was that her tank was on empty and she needed some petrol to get there, but she had left her purse at home.

I was surprised by the cashier's response. He said no, if she wanted any petrol she would have to pay for it now. The woman pleaded that she would bring the money down as soon as she returned from the medical centre. He still refused. She only wanted $10 worth, and given the circumstances I thought he should have agreed. Seeing her plight, I offered her $10 to get her going, but she refused. I insisted that she would make my day if she accepted the offer and after a bit more cajoling she finally accepted.

I left that petrol station with two things going through my mind: how great it felt to assist someone in need just like that, and how I wouldn't be returning to that petrol station again. That cashier has lost more than $10! Now you might be thinking that if he gave every person credit, he would be broke. Well, I believe we all have the power to detect fraudulent behaviour. If we are in touch with our feelings, we can tell when someone is having us on. And I could tell that this woman was as honest as tomorrow follows today.

Claudia Extols the Virtues of Giving

Claudia wrote to me after reading *The Mini Motivator*, saying she had loved my suggestion to pay for the car behind her next time she was at a tollgate: 'As soon as I read that, I decided that every Friday morning from then on I would pay the Harbour Tunnel toll for the car behind me. Nearly every time, the person in the car has got out, raced up beside me and thanked me. That $2 investment is amazing value for money – the look on the other drivers' faces is priceless! I also get a free kick out of it and find myself looking forward to Friday mornings with anticipation.'

And all for two dollars!

He Gave Up His Business-class Seat

Gus, a frequent flyer by anyone's language, was on his usual Sydney/Melbourne/Sydney weekly trip when he noticed an opportunity to give something away to a total stranger. Well, not a *total* stranger.

Gus had already taken his seat in business class, and was watching people as they boarded the plane just in case he knew someone. To his surprise, one of his favourite TV stars came aboard. He hoped the person would sit next to him, but he just kept walking past. To Gus's surprise, the star walked into economy class and sat down at the back of the plane. Gus was shocked.

As the seat next to him was vacant, he decided to ask the flight purser whether he could invite the TV star to come and sit there. Just as Gus was approaching the purser, the last passenger boarded the plane – and you guessed it, he sat in the empty seat. Gus was cheesed off. He had had it all worked out. The purser shut the door and the cabin crew proceeded to demonstrate the safety features of the plane.

Then Gus had an idea. He asked the purser if he could *swap seats* with the TV star. The purser thought Gus was joking at first, but when he realised he was serious, he said, 'No problem.' When the star got to Gus's seat, the purser explained that the person who had given up his seat was one of the star's biggest fans and had offered the seat to say thank you for the years of entertainment he and his family and friends had enjoyed.

About two weeks later, when Gus had all but forgotten about the incident, a letter arrived from the TV star thanking him for his generosity. Enclosed were four tickets to the taping of a TV special in which the star was appearing.

What goes around comes around!

How Can He Afford All Those Lunches?

When I was building my business, I decided that the only way to get enough time with prospective clients was to take them out for lunch. I'm not talking about a boozy, 'eighties-style' lunch, but a two-course, one-and-a-half-hour business lunch where we could discuss my proposal without constant interruptions. Everyone has to have lunch, I reasoned.

Gossip eventually gets back to the person who is being targeted. One Saturday evening I was a guest at a dinner party and the subject of entertaining clients came up. Someone mentioned that they had recently heard someone question how I could afford to take my clients out to fancy restaurants when my business was still in its infancy.

I was a bit taken aback, but explained that I was doing it because I believed in the principle of 'What goes around comes around'. I knew that if I could persist for long enough in my business, it would only be a matter of time before my clients were returning the favour by giving me business or taking me out to lunch themselves.

Let me qualify something here straight away. I never took someone to lunch or dinner expecting to get a meal in return. I just knew in my heart that 'What you sow, so shall you reap'. I was sowing a lot of seeds and they would definitely sprout one day into fully grown flowers – that is, new business. And guess what? I was right. Not only are my current clients providing heaps of business for me, they also enjoy having a meal with me now and again to discuss further possibilities.

In the early days of my career I didn't see a business lunch as 'giving', but it sure is. How much have you 'given away' in your business lately?

Restaurants Love Tips

One of the fascinating features of travelling overseas is that you experience different cultures and 'ways of life'. If you have travelled to the USA, you would have faced the task of 'tipping' – from taxi drivers to hairdressers, waiters to bellhops. It's a part of life in America that when you receive pretty good service, you give 10 to 15 per cent on top of the bill (a 'gratuity').

Why am I writing about tips in a chapter on giving and receiving? Well, the tip is a way of saying how much you appreciated the great service provided to you. Service is a 'product', just like any other. In Australia, I am amazed how many of us resist giving a good tip to someone who has provided excellent service. We have all had special occasions ruined because someone who was supposed to provide service forgot, or simply couldn't be bothered. Comments such as 'No way, this is not the States', 'We've paid the bill' and 'They've charged us enough already' simply reinforce people's lack of understanding of this brilliant, yet so often misunderstood element of giving.

As part of my consulting, I frequent restaurants in all the major capitals in Australia. A good restaurant is no different to any other successful business: the quality of the service you receive will always be high and the delivery of that service always professional. But for me, nothing beats the feeling of taking a special client to a restaurant I know well. Everyone in the place receives good service, but who do you think gets outstanding service? Whose little whims are always taken care of? That's right, mine! As a way of saying I appreciate their efforts, I always provide a decent tip – which ensures that the next time I go there, I get the table I want, with the view ... and what goes around comes around!

If you go to a hairdresser, restaurant, bar or any other service provider regularly, watch what happens when you start tipping them a little bit extra for their service. It will come back in bucketloads. Everyone loves to be appreciated, so the next time you are preparing to pay a bill, ask yourself how much more you could add on to tell the person that you respect them and have enjoyed their service. It will be one of the best business decisions you make!

What Relationship Could Do with a Dose of Giving?

While 'giving to receive' is powerful in business, it can also be a strong element in personal relationships you may be trying to improve. Just as giving in business has its rewards, so too does giving in any relationship.

There Can Never Be Enough Red Roses in a Relationship

Troy, a fourth-year apprentice, attended one of my seminars recently. He had married young and was now in his third year of marriage, but he and his wife, Nina, were finding the going tough. Troy said that what he had picked up more than anything else in my seminar was how much he had let the 'little surprises' slowly die out of their relationship.

He told me, 'During the first two years after the wedding I was always coming home with a surprise. Sometimes it would be flowers and other times it would be a box of Nina's favourite chocolates. But over the past year we've slipped into ''work'' mode and we're starting to become very boring. We've even started to rent videos on the weekend instead of going out to the cinema and enjoying a meal before or after the film. We used to only hire videos on cold and wet midweek evenings!'

Troy wrote to me several weeks after the seminar to advise that his and Nina's relationship was now back on track, and that 'giving and receiving' was alive and well again in their home.

How is it where you live?

Want to know more about...?

14

Accepting compliments – and giving them too

People ask you for criticism, but they only want praise.

W. SOMERSET MAUGHAM

In this chapter:

◆ Sporting losses and their link to compliments

◆ Letting kids know that it's okay to accept compliments

◆ David's story – perfectionism and its link to love

◆ Why compliments can be very powerful in the workplace

◆ The Self-esteem Bank Account and compliments

◆ Say the magic words – 'Thank you' – then *shut up*!

One of the major hurdles to achieving success is recognising that you deserve compliments. By this stage of *Believe and Achieve!* you know the absolute power of self-esteem and how it controls your life. Top achievers know that they need to stay on top of the setbacks which are coming their way, and that in order to do this they need an 'armory' – and that armory is their Self-esteem Bank Account. One of the quickest ways to make deposits into your Self-esteem Bank Account is to start accepting the compliments people offer you.

How do you respond when someone pays you a compliment? Do you shrug your shoulders and feel embarrassed? Or do you hold your head high and say those two magic words: 'Thank you'? It's worth having a look at how your family conditioning has affected your ability or lack of ability to feel worthy of compliments. Many of us have been told to act 'humble' and never show that we expect a compliment.

It's Okay to Win … and It's Okay to Acknowledge It

The behaviour of some sportspeople after a win amazes me. Many times, I have seen a winning team captain interviewed on TV, and instead of playing up the win and building the self-confidence of the team, he or she focuses on the mistakes they made and says something like 'We were fortunate that the opposition missed a few easy catches.'

I can never work out why they do this. Maybe they think that if they play humble pie the media will go easy on them if they lose their next match. (I've got news for them!) It must come as a big surprise to them when they walk out onto the field the following week and get thrashed. When I hear a sportsperson playing down a win, I always make a point of watching their next performance. Very often they either lose outright or deliver a pretty mediocre performance.

I think the real reason why sportspeople say such things is that they think, 'If I accept compliments as if I deserve them, others will think I have a big head.'

I'm not saying that accepting compliments will make a team win matches, but I do think it could stave off form loss. By 'form loss' I simply mean a loss of confidence. No matter which way you cut it, when a cricket/tennis/football star loses form, 99.9 per cent of the time it is due to lack of personal confidence. I have had the privilege of consulting to sport stars, and the one thing I know for sure is this: if their self-confidence starts to lift, so does their performance.

The tricky part is that the loss of confidence may not be related to events on the sports field. It could be a personal matter such as their marriage stalling, or a sickness or death in the family. These sorts of events can shake the person so much that they are thinking about their life and their priorities more than their sport. As a result, their concentration on the field suffers.

Let Your Kids Know that It's Okay to Accept Compliments

Among the thousands of letters I received from readers of *You Can Do It!* were many from parents who said that they now realised they were passing on to their kids some of the outdated beliefs that *their* parents had given them. Many of these letters talked about accepting compliments.

One letter was from Cassie, who wrote, 'The penny has just dropped as to why I have always struggled with my self-esteem. For as long as I can remember, I was always "cut down to size" by my parents, especially my father. Any time something good happened, like I got excellent school results, my father would say what a load of rubbish school was and that it wasn't going to make me successful. "Only hard work will make you successful," he would proclaim. Of course, this made me feel useless, and I would wonder why I should bother working so hard if my only reward was constant bagging by Dad.

'What scares me more than anything is that I've realised I'm doing exactly the same thing – "cutting down" my own three kids when they come home from school to say they've done well in some class or other. My husband and I are now making a big effort to try and find something every day that each of the kids has done right. It's not an easy task, but at least we're focusing on the positive, not the negative like we were raised to.'

Perfectionism and Compliments

David is a senior executive for a large multinational corporation based in Brisbane. He told me he could never work out why he was so pedantic about having everything 'just right'. After reading *You Can Do It!*, he realised that it was due to his strict upbringing – especially his mother's insistence that everything had to be perfect 'or you won't receive any love from me!' While this was never said in so many words, it's a familiar story. Many people who see themselves as perfectionists would agree with David's theory.

Melinda, who was in one of my Perth seminars, said she had always thought that being a perfectionist meant that she had a higher level of expectation than everyone else. But after many years battling depression and stress, she now realises that perfectionism has less to do with doing the job better than everyone else than wanting acceptance and love from her family and friends. She said that her conditioning was from the 'never good enough' school, where everything she did or attempted to do was criticised by her parents – thus her never-ending chase for acceptance and approval.

Kids who grow up without compliments never really know how they are doing. They never have the opportunity to feel that they are worthwhile, and many of them subsequently turn into adults with low self-esteem who constantly 'scream out' for acceptance.

Perfectionism and Compliments in the Workplace

One of the most asked questions in my corporate seminars is, 'If I demand a high standard of myself, why shouldn't I expect my staff to rise to that standard?'

It's a great question, but many people who ask it have missed the point. They think that people who don't measure up to their own high standard are slack. But what is really going on is this: it's not that others can't measure up; the problem is that the managers who ask the question **haven't managed to convince their staff that they can achieve the higher standard**.

If the staff knew they could do better, they would be doing so right now. No staff member gets out of bed in the morning intending to cheese the boss off – they want to give more. It takes good leadership to develop people's belief in themselves and encourage them to lift their standards.

The Self-esteem Bank Account and Compliments

It's appropriate to revisit the Self-esteem Bank Account concept here. It's relevant because it's related to the saying 'You can't give away something you don't already have.' In this case that something is self-esteem. How can you find positive features in your family and friends if you haven't found them in yourself? Remember, the world is your mirror and the people in it reflect how you are currently feeling.

Make a point right now to start lifting your Self-esteem Bank Account so you can pay compliments to others easily and genuinely. No one likes a cheap or insincere compliment, but when it's from the heart, the recipient feels the power and intent – and what a great feeling that is!

Learn How to Say the Magic Words

You can receive every compliment in the world, but if you don't feel you deserve them, you will always be looking for reasons to reject them. Some people do this by becoming all embarrassed and saying things like 'It was nothing', or not saying anything at all. Others behave in a more aggressive manner, muttering comments such as 'I wonder what *he* wants?' or 'She must be up to something.' These sorts of responses infer that you don't deserve compliments as a normal part of your life – you think something is wrong with being complimented.

You have to get used to accepting compliments in the same way that you have become used to deflecting them when they are given to you. Accepting compliments is really accepting that the world thinks you are awesome. If you keep on deflecting them, somehow they will stop arriving! Let me show you what I mean.

Maggie, a lawyer's receptionist, told me she understood this point very well. 'By rejecting the compliments, I was actually telling people to stop giving them to me. In my job I try to dress well every day. When I first started at the firm, everyone would tell me how smart I looked or how impressed they were with my choice of colour, and so on. I would respond with a throw-away line like, "Oh, I just grabbed anything I could", which I now realise was a really dumb thing to say as in reality I used to spend at least an hour getting myself ready for work. I deserved those compliments!'

Maggie realised that it's in her best interests to say just two words when a compliment comes her way: 'Thank you'!

Like Maggie, you could be conditioning your friends, family and work colleagues to stop complimenting you. How accepting have you been when they have paid you a compliment? How do you think others feel when they compliment you? Are their comments met with a cheerful 'Thanks heaps', or do you tend to justify why you don't deserve the compliment?

You now know that you deserve every compliment you get. And every time you accept one, your self-esteem will grow, as will your expectations of what is good enough for you.

Thank you are two words that can make a huge difference in your life – but only *you* can decide whether you will use them or not.

Want to know more about...?

15

You can be charismatic too!

You attract whatever you think you deserve.

PAUL HANNA

In this chapter:

- How charisma can be created but not faked

- Charisma is more than looks

- The golden smile – how many times a day do you use it?

- Thinking right towards people creates charisma

- Pushy salespeople and charisma

- Charisma and relationships

- Alan's story – looking for the woman of his dreams

W hy is it that when some people walk into a room, no one there bats an eyelid? Other people can walk into the very same room, and bang! They stop everyone in their tracks.

Charisma, or aura, is the unmistakable quality that turns actors into celebrities, makes an everyday salesperson the star performer in an organisation, and separates the mistrusted politician from the adored statesman. Charisma is a quality you can gradually create, if you believe in your heart of hearts that you deserve more – if you believe in your heart that people are fantastic.

You can create charisma, but you can't fake it. There is something inside us that can detect whether someone is authentic or phoney. Don't ask me what it is, but I know we all have it. And anyone who thinks they can fake charisma doesn't understand its link to self-esteem and to **being at peace with yourself**. By this I mean being happy with who you are, warts and all. Charisma is not race- or gender-specific, nor is it to do with height or eye colour. I believe charisma is a brilliant resource we all have but which few people ever tap into.

Charisma is More than Great Looks

To get a handle on charisma, you need to look at life as it really is – no movies, no soap operas, just everyday life as it is. The biggest difference between the world of Hollywood and our own world is that successful people in all walks of life look just like you and me. They're just normal people, but they have managed to 'go within' and develop their power of charisma, and project it to the world. When they look in the mirror they don't just see their outer reflection – they know that deep down, they are awesome, they really count.

When you walk into a room full of people, do you feel scared and vulnerable? Or do you know that you have a lot to give to the people around you? At the beginning of a seminar I am walking into a room full of people I don't know – when I come to think of it, it's usually an *auditorium* full of people! I used to feel daunted by this because my selfconsciousness made me feel inadequate. Was my suit pressed correctly? Was I overweight?

What changed my perception was an article I read in a magazine, which said something like 'Always remember: when you walk into a room full of people, don't think of yourself.' That's right, 'don't think of yourself'. Your thoughts can be your demons, or they can be your friend. When you walk into a room full of people you don't know, focus your thinking on what you can do for them. Convince yourself that there are people in that room who really want to listen and learn from you. Know that they will find you to be a very special person.

The Golden Smile – How Many Times a Day Do You Flash It?

When I was working as a marketing executive with Qantas and travelling abroad to do business, there were occasional problems with language difficulty or illness, and sometimes I would desperately need a favour from someone. At such times, I knew I could always count on a smile to get me out of a jam. It immediately broke down barriers and I would find people only too willing to help me.

On the subject of smiles, when was the last time you saw a politician walk in front of a camera with a long face? At politician school (only joking!) they are told over and over again always to smile, no matter what. They know the public has so much mistrust for them anyway that it's always going to be hard to get their message across in five seconds on the evening news – but it will be even tougher if they don't smile.

We have all been blessed with this great tool for success. I'm not saying you need a smile like Tom Cruise or Claudia Schiffer, but I do know that very few of us use this dynamic feature to illuminate our personality and encourage people to warm to us. If you want to be treated better than you are currently being treated, make it a practice to smile so many times a day. Like everything, the more you do it, the more comfortable you will become with it – and then the more you will do it, and so on.

Think Right Towards Other People

Because charisma is 99 per cent in your mind (that is, it is not dependent on how you look), how you think towards other people will have a dramatic effect on how powerful your charisma is. How charismatic you come over to others will largely depend on how you are currently thinking towards those people.

During my early days as a speaker, when things were not going so well in my business, I could predict whether a certain day was going to be positive, with a contract or two landed, or negative, with no business, by how I was feeling. Could it be that my prospective clients were picking up vibes from me? Maybe they could tell when I expected to be successful in getting their business and when I didn't think I had a chance.

Many high-achieving salespeople tell me that they have experienced this phenomenon to some degree or other. They tell me their 'war stories' – about how they turned their business around the moment they started taking accountability for their thinking and realised that it *was* affecting others and *was* contributing to their success or failure.

Breaking the Stereotype of Pushy Salespeople

Marilyn is a successful real-estate agent who knows all about charisma. She learnt about it not long after she went through a messy divorce. She told me that when she first entered the real-estate game, she shared other people's beliefs about real-estate salespeople – they're pushy, they never listen, they sell you things you don't really want and, worst of all, they rip you off. My experience has taught me that these are not truths. They are myths about people who work in an industry dealing with a highly emotive product: the home you are going to live in for years to come.

Marilyn has a warm personality and an infectious laugh. She was offered her job by a good friend, Jack, who thought her style would relax people while they were making one of the biggest decisions of their lives. Jack was right – more or less! He was right about Marilyn's style, but didn't know that she held some outdated beliefs about her job, and that these beliefs were blocking her charisma from shining through.

Marilyn's first four months showed only slow sales, so one day she sat down with Jack over a coffee and asked him what he thought her problem was. Jack said, 'When we ran that house inspection the other day, I noticed that you were quite pushy with that young couple. Afterwards I heard the woman tell her partner that she didn't want to attend the auction because she found your style too aggressive.'

After her chat with Jack, Marilyn realised she was letting her beliefs about real-estate salespeople get in the way. She had won many sales awards in a previous job in a large department store, and knew she had charisma. If she could just be herself, she knew she could connect with people easily.

Two years have passed since then and Marilyn is, as they say in the industry, 'pumping'. She has not only achieved her budgets every month, but has exceeded them on many occasions. Marilyn said that she always knew she had the sales skills and the desire to succeed, but what made her a star performer was allowing her charismatic self to come to the fore.

Charisma and Relationships

Most people are influenced by Hollywood when it comes to what they view as 'right' or 'perfect' in their relationships. If you turn on the TV at any time, you see programs with the 'beautiful people' acting their way to riches. I have no problem with this – I love going to the movies and watching, say, the latest James Bond film with all its outrageous stunts and props. But when I leave, I don't jump into my car and try to do what 007 does. I know it's just a film, and that is part of the escapism of the cinema. The danger is when you blur the line between what's 'Hollywood' and what's real.

Alan Looks for the Woman of His Dreams

Alan, a manager, came up to me at the end of a half-day seminar. He said he was really taken aback with what he had heard and could we meet for a coffee. He didn't know that his boss had already booked all his top managers, including Alan, into individual consultancy sessions with me.

When I met him about a month later, Alan told me that he had had problems meeting 'Ms Right' and was wondering whether this could have something to do with his charisma. I asked him what he thought and he said, 'I've been putting too much emphasis on finding a "dream babe" instead of a companion for life. I hadn't realised how much I've been affected by the unrealistic images on TV and in the movies. I've always been told I have a great personality, but I realise I haven't been letting it show because I'm always questioning whether the girl is good enough.'

Some time after our discussion I spoke to Alan again. He told me he is making progress in meeting women because he has seen that his unrealistic expectations have been preventing his charisma from shining through. He is now more relaxed and his close friends have noticed that he isn't putting people down as much – especially women he meets socially.

Charisma is a powerful component of life and can be the deciding factor in whether you become successful or not. Remember, we all have it. Like Alan, maybe all you need is to remove some of those self-imposed barriers to let your real personality shine through.

Want to know more about...?

16

Enjoying the moment

Yesterday is but today's memory and tomorrow is today's dream.

KAHLIL GIBRAN

In this chapter:

- ◆ Why focusing on the 'now' can propel you to the future

- ◆ How work promotions and commitment are connected

- ◆ Tommy – the best carwasher there is

- ◆ Deanne – the director of first impressions

- ◆ Why you don't have to win every argument

- ◆ Let people be who they are – you don't have to fix everyone

- ◆ Accepting your body, warts and all!

- ◆ Learn to say *no*!

C an you remember a time in your life when everything felt just great? Maybe it was during your childhood when you were on holidays, loving those endless days at the beach. Or maybe it was when you were walking back down the aisle with the partner of your dreams on your arm after saying those magic words, 'I do.' For some people it was when they were on holidays, lounging around poolside reading a great book, knowing they had at least two more weeks of doing the same thing!

Whenever the experience grabbed you, it was your decision to let go and enjoy the moment that was the defining element in achieving all that joy. Feeling the moment is simply absorbing the feeling of 'now'. It's feeling the sun on your back at the beach; it's watching the smiling faces as you walk back down the aisle; it's ordering another mango daiquiri when you know you shouldn't, but you only have to walk a few steps to reach your room at the resort. Enjoying the moment is all about enjoying what you are thriving on in the present in order to propel yourself into the future.

All entertainers need to master this major discipline. They must learn to focus on the performance they are giving now, and when it is over, look forward to future engagements booked in the diary. I see this every day when I completely immerse myself in whatever I'm doing, whether I'm consulting one-to-one or presenting to 500 people. If I get distracted and my focus shifts, it's very noticeable both to me and to my audience, who instinctively feel that I'm 'somewhere else'. But when I focus totally on the person or group in front of me, I enjoy every moment – and it shows. The time flies for them and for me and many attendees comment on how quickly the day has gone.

Can you think of a time when you completely lost yourself in what you were doing? Do you remember how quickly the time seemed to go? You looked at the clock and were amazed at how fast those hands had ticked.

Some Advice that Really Helped Me

We all get advice as we go through life. Some of it is useless, but some of it has the power to make a real difference and change your life. One such piece of advice, which I received during my teenage years, came from a wealthy businessman who used to call into our grocery shop every day to buy lunch. He always arrived in a very flash sports car, and as I have been a car buff for as long as I can remember, I always took notice when he arrived. One day in late 1975 – the year my father died – I was serving in the shop during the school holidays when he arrived in a gleaming red Porsche 911. I asked him, 'How do you become so successful that you can buy a new Porsche?'

I remember his reply word for word. 'Son,' he said, '**if you throw yourself into everything you do, the money will come**.'

At the time, I thought he meant that if you find the job of your dreams and really love doing it, the money will come. But that's not what he meant. He meant that if you throw yourself into every job you have, and fall in love with it, then the money will come.

There is a huge gap between the two interpretations. The first means that you search for a job which promises stacks of money and total autonomy to do what you like. Maybe you set up your own business. But many people fail in their own business because they think, by working for themselves and not having to take orders from anybody, they will make heaps of money and be less stressed out. Nothing could be further from the truth. If the buck stops with you, you will be the toughest boss in the world. You will have no excuses. The second interpretation means that if you commit yourself 100 per cent to whatever task you are doing, you can't help but become successful. Everyone notices those people who give much more than they have to and have a great time doing it. These are the ones who get promoted.

Many people give heaps at work and endure long hours, for no reward. In many cases, they play the martyr at work, letting everyone know how long they are working and what a burden it is. If you know that you do this, stop! No one enjoys whingers, and this sort of behaviour typecasts you as a loser who would not cope with any more responsibility – 'so how can we promote her?'

Here's what to do. From now on, focus all your energy into loving your work and enjoying the moment, by concentrating on the great people you work with and the lifestyle the job allows you to maintain. If you are thinking, 'But I hate the people I work with, and my lifestyle is lousy', it's about time you took another look at your self-esteem. It was your self-esteem that allowed you firstly, to accept this job and secondly, to stay in it. When you lift your self-esteem, one of two things will happen: either you will start to enjoy your work a whole lot more, or you will find something better and leave. Either way, it will be the right move for you.

Tommy, the Best Carwasher there is

I am reminded of the businessman's advice every time I have my car washed. On cold winter mornings and scorching summer afternoons, I see the principle being demonstrated before my very eyes. Tommy, my carwasher, is the ultimate professional. He encompasses everything the businessman meant when he said, 'Do what you love and the money will come.' Tommy is no millionaire, nor does he aspire to be one. His goals are more powerful than money. He said to me once that what motivates him to get out of bed in the early hours of the morning is that he knows his clients are relying on him to turn their dirty car into an immaculate show-piece which will not only look better, but enhance their image in the rough-and-tumble of the business world.

The way he dries the car with the chamois, vacuums the interior and shines the windows is a daily reminder to me that it takes just as much time to do a second-rate job as it does to do a first-rate one. The only difference is attitude! For Tommy, 'enjoying the moment' means not only doing a great job with the car, but revelling in meeting the people he comes into contact with every day. It means knowing that others depend on him to ensure that their vehicle looks immaculate, seven days a week. He could whinge about the early starts and cold mornings in winter or stinking hot days in summer, but instead he chooses to 'enjoy the moment'. And this manifests itself in the business he attracts by word of mouth – the best advertisement there is!

Director of First Impressions

Deanne is a receptionist at a large corporation. She was the first person I met when I arrived to speak to the managing director about conducting some seminars for his organisation.

About a month after I met her, Deanne attended one of my seminars. Later she told me how she had identified with the section on enjoying the moment. She said, 'A few months ago, I was getting upset and depressed about my job as a receptionist. I wanted to move to a position that was more ''respected'' in the organisation. Roger, the managing director, noticed my downbeat attitude and asked what was wrong. I told him I wanted to move on because I felt that the other staff and the customers didn't appreciate me.

'He listened to me and let me get everything out, and then said the magic words which changed my attitude forever: "I don't understand, Deanne. You are the director of first impressions! No other person in the organisation has the power to affect so many people on a daily basis."

'I never realised my role was so important. I immediately felt better, and the more I thought about it the more sense it made. Roger's comments helped me to understand that from then on I needed to throw myself into my job, because every phone call I answer and every client I greet at reception has the chance to make or break the company.'

Deanne finished by telling me that her self-esteem has gone through the roof – everyone has been complimenting her telephone manner and her style at the reception counter. With this new-found confidence she has decided to dress more smartly and professionally than ever before. She is really 'enjoying the moment' and loving her job – and she has just been invited to apply for the job of personal assistant to the sales director, who is most impressed with her new attitude and confidence.

Eight Tips to Assist You in Enjoying the Moment

1. You don't have to win every argument.

You might have heard the saying, 'To win the battle is not to win the war.' What this means, if you are having a disagreement with someone, is that you might win that particular argument, but the long-term damage you are doing to your relationship with that person could be a heavy price to pay.

The next time you have a disagreement with someone, take ten deep breaths and ask yourself if winning is worth the cost of damaging your relationship. I'm not asking you to be a 'doormat' who gets walked over all the time; I'm just reminding you to keep your eyes on your goals. If one of your goals is to maintain a loving relationship with your partner, or a harmonious relationship with your work colleagues, have a good look at the little points you are winning at the expense of achieving your goals.

2. Don't be a 'fix-it cop'.

Everyone on this planet is different and has different ways of navigating through life. It's easy to fall into the trap of being a 'fix-it cop', always looking for things that aren't perfect and insisting that they be changed. This will only highlight to others how inflexible you are. Try to look at things you would normally want to change as a lesson in acceptance. Fashion, food, racial identity – these are all different because they are what makes the world go round.

The next time you feel compelled to make people conform to your preferred style, take ten deep breaths and thank your lucky stars that not only is this person different, but that they are in Australia and free to express themselves without fear. Millions of people would cherish this freedom, yet we take it for granted. If you want to bring peace into your world, try to accept people and their quirks as part of life, and not as faults that have to be corrected.

3. Achieve to please yourself instead of others.

How much are you seeking approval from others? Are you constantly doing things just to please them? For example, you might be having a relationship with a person from a particular race or profession because it pleases others more than it pleases you. Perhaps you are following the same career as your mother, father, brother or sister because they want you to uphold the family tradition in medicine, law, plumbing or building. This is not the way to success. Make your own mind up and run with it.

4. Accept your body for who you are now.

I don't think I have met a person on this planet – male or female – who is 100 per cent happy with their body. Some want to be thinner; others want bigger breasts or stronger pecs; some must have the 'Melrose' look for their nose, lips, eye colour or hair. While I think it's great to want to look better, the irony is that one of the first steps required on any self-improvement program is a belief in yourself. You must first believe that you are okay, and this will spark your determination to achieve.

5. Don't play 'catch-up' with the Joneses.

You have heard the saying 'keeping up with the Joneses'. How many times do you find yourself under pressure because you are trying to outdo or overtake someone? It's great to want to strive for a better car or house, but first make sure your intention is right – that is, that you are doing it for your own need to achieve, and not to try to outdo someone else.

6. Bring a bit more impulsiveness into your world.

I am the first to advise that we must all have goals to strive for, but living life too predictably can starve your creative power. Introduce some unpredictability into your life and watch your excitement grow. Try taking in a movie on a night you would normally stay at home, or going away for a weekend on the coast when your plans were to spend your usual 'plod around the house' weekend.

7. Learn to say no.

Learning to say no without feeling guilty can really assist you in enjoying the moment. Too many times, when you just want to veg out and be by yourself, you feel compelled to attend that family gathering or show up at that dinner with friends. These occasions are great most of the time, but not when your mood says, 'Chill out.' The next time you don't feel like going, say so – and watch your contentment level rise.

8. *Have a dinner party or barbecue.*

Sometimes we need to take charge not only of our life, but of the lives of others – not in a personal sense, but in a party sense. No successful dinner party or barbecue happens out of thin air. It starts with an idea, which is followed by hard work, which then delivers a great day.

So how does having a dinner party or barbecue relate to enjoying the moment? Easy! When you have all your friends around you and you're having a great time, you will experience the true message of this chapter – which is to enjoy every moment as if it's your last.

Want to know more about...?

17

Non-judgement – no longer judging others

Walk a mile in another Indian's moccasins before you make judgement.

NATIVE AMERICAN SAYING

In this chapter:

- ◆ Judith's story – chilling out towards her teenage son
- ◆ See your kids as always improving – and they will!
- ◆ Race, sex and discrimination – how we have changed as a nation
- ◆ The doner kebab that shocked
- ◆ Non-judgement and travelling abroad

W hen you have worked on yourself, and mastered some of the techniques included in other chapters, you will be ready for this chapter. I say this because, out of all the material covered in this book and in *You Can Do It!*, I think this chapter has awesome power to help you achieve much more in your life. It's about 'non-judgement' – about making changes on the inside and letting people and things outside of you travel through life at their own speed.

Judith Chills Out Towards Her Teenage Son

It's well known that parents and teenagers often talk to each other on different wavelengths, not really hearing what the other person is saying. Judith, a personal assistant to one of my clients, shared this story with me recently.

Judith really loves her job, depite the fact that she is required to keep long hours in the office. She knew this when she applied for it 12 months ago, but has lately been finding it tough going – not from a corporate point of view, but on the home front, where she is constantly clashing with her 15-year-old son, Josh.

Judith said she really liked the part in my seminar where I talked about non-judgement. She had immediately thought of Josh.

She said, 'I've never seen myself as overbearing, but on reflection I think I might have been cramping Josh's emotional space. He's 15 now, and wants to find his way in the world, but says he feels I'm always watching over his shoulder.'

This habit of Judith's had created an air of mistrust between her and Josh, which resulted in them 'having words' and not speaking to each other for a couple of days. She said, 'At work, listening is my most powerful skill when it comes to assisting my boss, who is super-busy and doesn't suffer fools gladly. But at home, it's a different story. I realised that I rarely listen to Josh, and still expect him to jump to attention like he did when he was small.'

Judith said that the most important point she learnt about non-judgement was that if she could think of Josh as always improving, and keep on reinforcing this to him, he would eventually come around. On the other hand, if she keeps on doing what she is currently doing, always pointing out what he is doing wrong, he will rebel even further and the next call she receives might be from the police.

She said that my statement, '**When you give people answers, you take away their power**', had really hit home: 'I know now that picking up after Josh and making all the tough decisions for him is only going to make him more dependent on me instead of helping him grow up as an independent adult. I've seen this in my sister's son, who was spoilt from day one. He has grown up insecure about his own ability to make the right decision about most things, and still runs to his parents for reassurance at the age of 25. From now on I'm focusing all my energy on listening more to Josh and accepting him for who he is, not what I want him to be.'

Race, Sex and Discrimination

I received my education in the seventies, in a school system that was very Anglo-Saxon. I didn't have a problem with this; my parents had gone to school here in Australia too and our upbringing wasn't your typical 'wog' style. I mean, we did eat some 'wog food', but basically everything else was very 'Anglo'.

An amazing thing happened on the first day of one school term. Up to this point, there was me and maybe two other guys who were from an ethnic background, but we were Anglo enough to melt into the pack and thereby avoid getting picked on. At lunch time on this day, one of the new kids, who was from a Lebanese background, pulled his lunch out of his lunchbox. I nearly died. I couldn't believe it. He had a doner kebab with houmous and tabouli! I jumped to my feet immediately and said to him, 'What the hell are you doing? Do you want to get us bashed up?'

How times have changed. Walk through any shopping mall today and you will not only see a full range of Lebanese food, but also Thai, Turkish, Mexican and just about any other taste you fancy. Australia has come a long way since the 1970s in the area of tolerance and non-judgement. But if we are to extend our great record, we need to ensure that everyone 'chills out' a bit and learns to be comfortable firstly with who they are. Once this is accomplished the rest will flow on.

This is why I think every Australian should be travel overseas at least once in their life. People who have travelled extensively are rarely racist and usually very willing to try new things. And that's what travel is all about: broadening the mind and allowing us to celebrate each other's differences without feeling threatened by them.

I Learnt About Non-judgement in Asia

One of the highlights of my working career has been having the opportunity to visit Asia on a regular basis. In my job at Qantas, I had to deal with every facet of holidays in Asia, from China to Thailand, Bali to Hong Kong, India to Japan. What a melting pot – but what a learning experience.

My number-one rule when travelling anywhere in the world – not only Asia – is to 'chill out' and 'live and let live'. If you start judging everything by Australian standards, you will end up having a nightmare of a trip. Everything is different – the smells, the sounds, the traffic, the customs, the food and even the sense of humour. When I was in Asia I was always impressed by people's attitude to work and attention to detail. From five-star hotels to a little *barong* (restaurant) in Bali, they were all proud of what they did and welcomed you in like a long-lost family member.

But this chapter is all about non-judgement, right? Non-judgement is what I saw in each country I visited. The people forgave the stupid comments they heard and the dumb questions many tourists asked, to ensure that you enjoyed your holiday. It was complete non-judgement at work.

You can achieve much more happiness in your life if you start to focus less on differences and instead try to appreciate other people for their beautiful uniqueness. Make a commitment right now to give your best effort to accepting others for who they are. You will be surprised at how this acceptance will end up coming back to you.

Want to know more about…?

18

What would your epitaph say?

What lies before us and what lies beyond us is tiny compared to what lies within us.

HENRY DAVID THOREAU

In this chapter:

- ◆ Having a good rethink about what you're doing with your life
- ◆ Richard and Olivia's story – a 40th birthday in Paris
- ◆ Len's story – General Manager and now better father
- ◆ Martina's story – I never finish anything
- ◆ Grant's story – Mr Gunna!

I t might feel a bit morbid to talk about what would be written on your gravestone, but after my mother's near-death accident (see Chapter 9) I must admit I had a good look at myself and asked myself some tough questions.

Have I really made a difference on this earth if I were to go tomorrow? Is there anyone whom I have hurt, that I could make amends with? Is my time properly divided between my business and my family and friends? Is there anything I keep on saying I would like to try or a place that I have always wanted to visit, but have kept on making excuses and therefore not achieved any results in these areas? How could I improve my health?

These are just some of the questions that have caused me to have a good rethink about where I am heading and how I am going to get there. The toughest question you can ask yourself is, 'What will my epitaph say?' It really does make you have a good look at your life and the quality – or lack of quality – in it at the moment.

No More Excuses, We are Going to Paris!

Richard attended my seminar with a major financial institution, on the Central Coast of New South Wales. At the end of the seminar, I posed the 'epitaph' question. Richard was quite amazed. He found the question thought-provoking and told me that the one thing that came to his mind was Paris.

I asked, 'Paris, as in France?', and he said, 'Absolutely.'

You see, Richard and his wife, Olivia, had always talked about going to Paris to celebrate her fortieth birthday. They were both dinki-di Aussies and had no French relatives or anything like that; they had just always wanted to visit Paris, as it seemed like the world's most romantic destination. Richard said, 'While we've always talked about it, in the back of our minds there's a little voice questioning the logic of spending thousands of dollars travelling to Paris when for the same money we could update the car or extend our home and also have a holiday in Tahiti.'

About six months later, I had the privilege of conducting a follow-up seminar for the same organisation. Richard came up to me with a big grin. He and Olivia had just returned from a six-week holiday in Europe – and guess where they spent Olivia's fortieth birthday? In a beautiful restaurant on the Champs Elysées in Paris! Richard said that when I had asked the group to write their own epitaph, a massive feeling of compulsion had welled up inside him. 'When you asked that question, I suddenly thought, "I'll never forgive myself if we reach old age and are still justifying why we can't afford to go to Paris." When I got home that night, I went straight to Olivia and said, "Let's go to Paris." And that was that. It was more than we ever imagined – and we're planning a return visit in two years.'

Richard finished by saying, 'Paris was always waiting for us. We just had to believe in ourselves and commit to it.'

A New Epitaph: A New Person

Recently I was speaking at a major Australian company's sales kick-off in the Blue Mountains, west of Sydney. The marketing director had read *You Can Do It!* and had booked me to speak at the conference. After I had finished my presentation, I was signing some books at the back of the room when a guy approached me who introduced himself as Len. He gave me his book to autograph, saying he had enjoyed my presentation very much and would I have a cup of tea with him after I finished the signings. I agreed to meet him later.

The next person in the queue was Terri. As I was signing her book, she said I had made quite an impression on the 'big boss'. I asked who that was and she said it was Len, the guy I had just met!

About half an hour later I sat down with Len over some peppermint tea and he told me again how much he had enjoyed my presentation. He had come up the ranks through the company, as most people his age did, learning the ropes and creating a network of loyal workers and a committed management team. He went on to say that he had heard many speakers presenting pretty much the same stuff as me, but that no one had ever spoken about 'Your Epitaph'. He said that as I was speaking, his thoughts had rushed home to his family and how much they had put up with over the years.

He said, 'I always wanted to become general manager, and achieving this two years ago not only gave me great satisfaction, but enabled me to enhance my family's lifestyle with the purchase of a new house. But I started to think about how little time I've spent with my wife and kids since I became general manager. I realised that I don't want to leave this planet with my epitaph reading that I was a great worker and provider but a lousy dad.'

Len said that he was determined to start immediately to rewrite his epitaph. About four months later I received a postcard from the Grand Canyon in Arizona, USA. It was from Len, who was writing to thank me for giving him the 'kick in the pants' he so badly needed. He said, 'After spending two weeks with my family I've realised what I've been missing out on!'

My Epitaph Would Say that I Never Finish Anything

Martina approached me after I had finished speaking at a seminar on the Gold Coast for her pharmaceutical company. She said she had been to many personal development seminars and always set her goals with good intentions. As she went on, though, she got bored with her goals and let them fall by the wayside.

She said, 'My epitaph would say that I always had good intentions but never quite had the courage to persist with my dreams. I've now made a decision to set one firm goal and go for it. I really want to be promoted from sales assistant to fully-fledged sales rep. I missed out on the last position and became quite negative towards the company, letting my personal presentation slip. I'm definitely behind the eight-ball now, but as of today I'm going to commit to my dream. Even if I don't get the job I want this time, at least I'll know that my epitaph will read that I was a persistent person who never gave up!'

Grant the 'Gunna'

Grant is a family friend pretty close in age to me who I knew when we were growing up. We lost contact for about ten years, as he moved to Melbourne with his father when his mother died.

Grant wrote to me to say how much he had enjoyed reading *You Can Do It!* and how thrilled he was with my success. He said that while we were both of similar age and education (very little!), there was one major difference between us. He was always 'gunna' do this or 'gunna' do that, but had never really committed to achieving any one thing in his life. He said he was always waiting for the 'big break' and that only now was he realising that there had been many 'big breaks' presented to him which he had squandered through his lack of focus and commitment.

Grant made one point that I will never forget. He said he was still young and had plenty of time to rewrite his epitaph: 'It's not over till the fat lady sings, and I'm going to turn over a new leaf from today on!'

If This Was My Last Six Months on Earth, I Would...

How would you end the sentence above? What would you make time for if you knew you had only six months to go on this planet? I know I might be sounding a bit downbeat, but I think it's good to have a 'reality check' now and again. Who said you are going to be here tomorrow or next year, anyway? There are no guarantees in life, and I like to constantly remind myself of the above sentence because it challenges me to start thinking about things I might be delaying or making excuses for not trying.

Try saying to yourself, '**If I had only six months to live, I would...**', then finish the sentence. You'll be amazed at how you start to run out of excuses!

It's Never Too Late to Change

We all have the opportunity to change our epitaph. It's never too late to rewrite it, and only you have the control. No one else has the power to do it. Make some quiet time over the next few days to have a good look at what might be written about you. Then put in place some changes that will leave a fitting epitaph to the awesome person you are.

Want to know more about…?

Concluding remarks

When I am on a plane, I tend to let my mind wander, moving from clients to family to friends to writing. On a recent flight I was reminded of just how impatient we can all be. Sitting right next to me was a woman with her 12-month-old baby son. I must admit that when they sat next to me I thought to myself, 'This is going to be fun. A screaming child all the way to Perth!'

But the little boy was an angel. He slept most of the way, and when he was not sleeping he was giggling and making faces at the crew and at me. He was a real entertainer – and his name was Jerry!

Soon that little boy will be embarking on one of his biggest missions in life: learning to walk. Have you ever seen a baby walk for the first time? If you have, you'll remember how determined it was, how it showed such belief in itself. You might also have been struck by the encouragement the baby received from its family – the kind of support we all wish would persist till our dying day.

There's another thing you might remember about this wonderful piece of theatre. The baby fell over! Did everyone start yelling at it and calling it a loser? No way. Everyone started to encourage it and, before you knew it, the baby was demolishing the lounge room!

Believe and Achieve! is fundamentally about 'walking again'. For so long you have been conditioned to accept where you are, or to be thankful for what you have in your life, but this is preventing your true potential from shining through. My sincerest wish at this point of *Believe and Achieve!* is that you now have a renewed belief in yourself and a determination to achieve bigger things both personally and at work.

Can you imagine what would happen to Jerry if his parents thought crawling around and making faces at everyone was good enough? Exactly! He would get to 30 and still be on his knees. In a way, you could be 'on your knees' in some areas of your life. Old beliefs you have accepted from years gone by could be crippling you in your personal, financial and work life. The exciting part about this is that you have done something about it, not only by investing in *Believe and Achieve!*, but also by reading to this point.

Now comes the biggest challenge: putting into action the concepts you have read about. It's a piece of cake, really! Let me explain. When I have been faced by a large task, I have looked at it as a large 'cake' which needs to be cut into pieces and then 'eaten' one piece at a time. So something that at first seemed very daunting becomes much easier to achieve.

For example, writing *You Can Do It!* and *Believe and Achieve!* are two of the biggest tasks I have undertaken, not only because they were large tasks in themselves, but because at the time of writing them, my speaking business was also going through the roof. But eventually, piece by piece – or chapter by chapter – the books were finished.

If you stew on a big job and keep delaying the start of it, you will never achieve any of it. Like the old saying goes: 'The journey of a thousand miles begins with one step.'

Finally, and more than anything else, never forget that there is only one 'you' on this planet, and that you have been put here to make a difference. No matter how hard life gets, or how many setbacks come your way, just remember the following quote from Calvin Coolidge, the 30th President of the USA.

Nothing in the world can take the place
of persistence.

Talent will not;
nothing is more common than
unsuccessful people with talent.
Genius will not;
unrewarded genius is almost a proverb.
Education will not;
the world is full of educated derelicts.

Persistence and determination alone
are omnipotent.

To laugh often and much;

To win the respect of intelligent people

and the affection of children;

To earn the appreciation of honest critics

and endure the betrayal of false friends;

To appreciate beauty;

To find the best in others;

To leave the world a bit better,

whether by a healthy child, a garden patch

or a redeemed social condition;

To know one life has breathed easier

because you have lived;

This is to have succeeded.

RALPH WALDO EMERSON

AMERICAN PHILOSOPHER, POET AND ESSAYIST (1803–82)

Suggested books and films

Reading books and seeing films always give me a great amount of food for thought. Here are some – both classics and recent ones – which have inspired me.

Books

Carnegie, Dale. *How to Win Friends and Influence People*. Simon & Schuster, 1981.

Diamond, Harvey & Marilyn, *Fit for Life*. HarperCollins, 1984.

Dowrick, Stephanie, *Forgiveness and Other Acts of Love*. Penguin, 1997.

Dyer, Wayne, *Your Sacred Self*. HarperCollins, 1995.

Hay, Louise L. *The Power is Within You*. Specialist Publications, 1991.

Hill, Napoleon & Stone, W. Clement. *Success Through a Positive Mental Attitude*. HarperCollins, 1990.

Jeffers, Susan. *Feel the Fear and Do It Anyway*. Arrow, 1987.

Kiyosaki, Robert. *Rich Dad, Poor Dad*. Techpress, 1997.

Mandino, Og. *The Greatest Miracle in the World*. Bantam, 1977.

Peale, Norman Vincent. *The Power of Positive Thinking*. Cedar, 1953.

Schuller, Robert. *Tough Times Never Last But Tough People Do*. Bantam, 1983.

Schwartz, David J. *The Magic of Thinking Big*. Simon & Schuster, 1987.

Stanton, Rosemary & Egger, Garry. *The Gutbuster Waist Loss Guide*. Allen & Unwin, 1998.

Films

Dead Poets Society (1989). Starring Robin Williams, Robert Sean Leonard and Ethan Hawke. Directed by Peter Weir. Touchstone.

The Doctor (1991). Starring William Hurt and Christine Lahti. Directed by Randa Haines. Touchstone.

8 Seconds (1994). Starring Luke Perry and Stephen Baldwin. Directed by John G. Avildsen. Newline Cinema.

Field of Dreams (1989). Starring Kevin Costner and Amy Madigan. Directed by Phil Alden Robinson. RCA/Columbia.

Good Will Hunting (1997). Starring Matt Damon, Robin Williams and Ben Affleck. Directed by Gus Van Sant. Roadshow.

Jerry McGuire (1997). Starring Tom Cruise and Cuba Gooding Jr. Directed by Cameron Crowe. Tristar Pictures.

Mr Holland's Opus (1995). Starring Richard Dreyfuss and Glenne Headley. Directed by Stephen Herek. Polygram.

My Life (1993). Starring Michael Keaton and Nicole Kidman. Directed by Bruce Joel Rubin. Roadshow.

Rudy (1993). Starring Sean Astin, Ned Beatty and Robert Prosky. Directed by David Anspaugh. Tristar Pictures.

The Shawshank Redemption (1994). Starring Tim Robbins and Morgan Freeman. Directed by Frank Darabont. Roadshow.

Shine (1996). Starring Geoffrey Rush, Armin Mueller-Stahl and Noah Taylor. Directed by Scott Hicks. 21st Century Pictures.

Stand and Deliver (1987). Starring Edward James Olmos and Lou Diamond Phillips. Directed by Roman Menendez. Warner.

When a Man Loves a Woman (1994). Starring Andy Garcia and Meg Ryan. Directed by Luis Mandoki. Touchstone.

Acknowledgements

As I write these acknowledgements, I am looking towards one of the most famous and beautiful structures ever built. When I look at the Sydney Opera House, I always think of the persistence, determination and vision that gave us this magnificent building, and the thousands of Australians who made it a reality. Now I'm not claiming that *Believe and Achieve!* is as momentous as this national icon, but like the Opera House, it has been possible because of the many 'construction workers' who have helped me make this book a reality.

PETER FIELD, the Managing Director of Penguin Books, who showed faith in an unknown author and was rewarded with a national number-one bestseller.

BOB SESSIONS, JULIE GIBBS and KATIE PURVIS, the architects behind the scenes at Penguin who continue to amaze me by their absolute commitment and professionalism. They know this business inside out!

PETER BLAKE, MARGARET THOMPSON and all the dedicated sales team at Penguin Books, the 'construction workers' who convinced the booksellers of Australia to stock *You Can Do It!* Without them, nothing would have happened. They are the true unsung heroes in this industry. Thanks heaps, guys. I will always remember your efforts.

GABRIELLE COYNE, the marketing wiz at Penguin, and her team in publicity: focused, dedicated and so well connected!

TOM PHILLIPS, STEVE LOTTER, RAY LAWSON, DANNY MILES, BERNIE SMITH and all the team at Toyota. What more can I say but . . . 'Oh, what a feeling!'

JOHN SYMOND, JAMES SYMOND and all the dynamos at Aussie Home Loans. I have enjoyed working with this company so much. After meeting their dynamic young team, you walk away convinced that they 'will save you'!

CHARLIE BELL, GUY RUSSO, RON MUSSALLI and all the team at McDonald's, who still blow my mind every time I get up in front of them. They really are the benchmark, not only in hamburgers, but in developing people and asking them to 'First believe, and then you will achieve.'

PETER ELWIN, who as General Manager of Qantas Flight Catering proved that if you believe in your people first, they will achieve. Unfortunately, as with many great talents before Peter, the world beyond Australia has seen his potential. He is now based in Hong Kong, heading one of the largest flight kitchens in the world. Thanks for all your help and commitment in the early days, Peter.

JOHN MCGRATH, whose unbelievable talent and vision created McGrath Partners. John has changed the rules in the real-estate game forever by delivering quality service that was previously unknown in the industry . . . and now the others are all playing catch-up! Good on you, John, and thanks for all your support.

CHRISTINE MAHER and all the team at Celebrity Speakers who have made the last 12 months so exciting. Christine knows the speakers' circuit better than anyone else in Australia, because she pioneered it! Thank you, Christine, for all your support.

TIM GILBERT, first cousin, best mate and producer at Channel Nine I grew up with Tim, and it's great to have someone with you on this journey who knows all your strengths and weaknesses. Right from the start, Tim *always* believed I would achieve. Thanks, TG!

GARY LECHTE, who is proof that when you truly believe in yourself you can achieve big things. Gary walks the talk every day and has the success – both financial and personal – to prove it! Thanks for being an inspiration, Gary.

To all my clients who have supported me over the years, especially PETER CAPP, KEN WRIGHT, HOWARD DAVY, ROBIN HONEY-CHURCH, JOHN MALOUF, WAYNE HANDLEY, NEIL SUTTON, GRAEME STEWART, KEN TAGG, DICK SIMPSON and TIM FARLEY.

MY FAMILY AND FRIENDS, who have always been there – through the tough times and now through the good times. They know the sacrifices required to write a book, because they are always on the receiving end of my long nights of writing or me missing family engagements. I cherish every moment we have together.

THE GILBERTS, Bill and Luerice, who were there with my mum during the touch-and-go hours after the accident. Not only were they there for her, but they have always been there for me. Thanks, Luerice and Bill. Also my close cousins Bill, Pat, Rob, Tim, Monica and Kieran. Every time we get together, the beautiful chemistry of love and mutual admiration flows. The Booker Bay days will always bond us!

NEIL GREGORY and ANDREW PAUL, my chiropractors, who have always been there to ensure that I maintain my stamina with this frenetic lifestyle. Thanks, guys.

WILLI MARTIN, GORDON FULLER and all the team at the PARK HYATT SYDNEY. All my clients agree – there is no hotel in Australia quite like the Park Hyatt. Everyone knows its location is awesome, but it's the warm, unpretentious service that keeps bringing everyone back – including me! Thanks, Willi and Gordon, for spoiling me and my guests *all the time*!

PETER CRINIS and his team at CROWN TOWERS MELBOURNE. Peter knows that the true reward of excellent service is repeat business. I can't wait till my next visit to Crown Towers – and all my clients agree on this, too. It's the only place to stay in Melbourne. We should all be proud of this truly world-class hotel.

Index

owning, conditioning about   152–3

Parable for Today, A   84–5
parents
    and belief systems   75–8
    blaming   12–13
    breaking away from   106–7
    conditioning by kids   84–6
    listening and non-judgement
      207–8
    perfectionism and conditional
      love   177–8
    role in conditioning   75–8
    see also children and family
parties, enjoying the moment   202
passion, nurturing   125–30
past mistakes, letting go of   36–7,
    156–60
past success in mental rehearsal   127
past, letting go of *see* non-attachment
perfectionism and compliments
    177–9
pessimists   14, 15
plateaus in weight loss   141–2
pleasing yourself   200
purpose in life
    breaking away   106–7
    connecting with   105–6
    courage and conviction   108–10
pushy salespeople stereotype   188–9
put-downs and self-image   11–14
putting up with things   92–5

race, non-judgement of   208–10
rear-vision thinking   25–8
relationships
    and appearance   79–80, 189–90

    being single   81–2
    and charisma   189–90
    enjoying the moment   118
    mid-life crisis   82–4
    and non-attachment   152–3, 154–6
    non-judgement   207–10
    rear-vision comments   26
    risk-taking   50–1
    saying no without guilt   201–2
    seeking approval   200
    setbacks and accountability   66–70
    steering-wheel comments   26
    and success   41–3
    winning arguments   199–200
    see also children and family;
      parents
repetition and calm   129
responsibility *see* accountability
restaurant tipping   168–9
risk-taking   49–56

saying no without guilt   201–2
school and education
    and non-attachment   159–60
    rear-vision comments   28
    steering-wheel comments   28
second-best scenario
    accepting   38–40, 92–4
    and mediocrity   22
seeking approval   200
self-belief
    expecting the best   21–3
    Field of Dreams   6–7, 8
    the means will arrive   128–9,
      151–2, 154
    and non-attachment   151–2
    and purpose in life   108–10

Nothing makes me happier than receiving a letter from a reader. I would love to hear your thoughts about *Believe and Achieve!, You Can Do It!* and *The Mini Motivator*. Please write to:

Paul Hanna
Believe and Achieve!
Private Bag 747
Church Point NSW 2105

or fax me on:
(02) 9999 0767

In this easy-to-read manual for success, Australia's leading motivational expert shows you how to achieve more of your potential. In *You Can Do It!* you will discover:

- How to set goals and focus on them
- How to boost your self-confidence
- How winners come back from defeat
- How to improve your kids' self-esteem
- How to deal with negative people
- How to maintain your momentum
- How to avoid plateauing out
- How to recharge your marriage
- How to attract the good things in life
- How to use your time off as a tool for success

The Mini Motivator is a handy collection of ideas to help you get motivated.

Use this book when you need a little bit of advice to get you going, keep you on track, or just lift your normal day out of the ordinary. It's an inspiration!